Stuart, John F. Smyth

A Tour in the United States of America, Volume 1

ISBN: 978-1-948837-11-8

This classic reprint was produced from digital files in the Google Books digital collection, which may be found at http://www.books.google.com. The artwork used on the cover is from Wikimedia Commons and remains in the public domain. Omissions and/or errors in this book are due to either the physical condition of the original book or due to the scanning process by Google or its agents.

This edition of John Stuart's **A Tour in the United States of America** was originally published in 1784 (London).

Townsends
PO Box 415, Pierceton, IN 46562
www.Townsends.us

A
TOUR
IN THE
UNITED STATES
OF
AMERICA:

CONTAINING

An Account of the PRESENT SITUATION of that Country;

The POPULATION, AGRICULTURE, COMMERCE, CUSTOMS, and MANNERS of the Inhabitants;

ANECDOTES of several MEMBERS of the CONGRESS, and GENERAL OFFICERS in the American Army;

AND

Many other very fingular and interefting Occurrences.

WITH

A Defcription of the INDIAN NATIONS, the general Face of the Country, Mountains, Forefts, Rivers, and the moft beautiful, grand, and picturefque Views throughout that vaft Continent.

LIKEWISE

Improvements in HUSBANDRY that may be adopted with great Advantage in EUROPE.

By *John* J. F. D. SMYTH, Esq.

VOL. I.

LONDON,

Printed for G. ROBINSON, Pater-nofter-Row; J. ROBSON, New Bond-Street; and J. SEWELL, Cornhill.

MDCCLXXXIV.

SUBSCRIBERS NAMES.

A

Lord Ashburton
William Pierce Ashe A'Court Ashe, esq. M.P.
John Allen, esq.
Thomas Ashwood, esq.

B

Duke of Buccleugh * †
Lord Viscount Beauchamp 2 *copies*
Sir Joseph Banks, bart. President of the Royal Society
Colonel Byde
Samuel Bagshaw, esq. of Ford
Owen Salisbury Brereton, esq. Vice-President of the Royal Society
Captain Bosville
W. H. Bevan, esq. Lincoln's Inn
Mr. William Butcher, Paradise-Row, Lambeth
Mr. Champion Bray, Manchester
Mr. John Blackwall, Blackwall

C

Earl of Carlisle
Earl Cornwallis
Lord Cathcart
Right Honourable H. S. Conway, M. P.
Sir Gray Cooper, bart. M.P. *
D. P. Coke, esq. M.P. 2 *copies*
P. G. Crauford, esq. F. R. S.

SUBSCRIBERS NAMES.

James Cotton, esq. late of North Carolina
Mr. Nicholas Creswell, Edale, Derbyshire, 3 *copies*
Mr. Peter Copland, James-street, Grosvenor-square
Mr. John Henry Carey, late of Maryland
A. C. 3 *copies*

D

Duke of Devonshire *
Earl of Dartmouth *
Earl of Dunmore
Sir J. Dyer, bart. *
Colonel Donald M'Donald, Highgate
Rev. Dr. Downes, Prebend of St. Patrick's, Dublin
Robert Dormer, esq. Duke-street, Westminster
T. Dyer, esq. *
Captain Henry Duncan, of the Royal Navy
Mr. Dennison, Duke-street, Manchester-square

E

Right Honourable William Eden, M. P. *
Honourable Thomas Erskine, M. P. * †

F

William Frazer, esq. Under Secretary of State
T. Freemantle, esq.
Captain Frazer, Coldstream Reg. of Guards
Captain Freemantle, ditto
Mr. Fisk
Mr. Septimius Furnis, Macclesfield
Mr. Richard Falkner, Sheffield
Mr. Charles Fox, Cornwall †

SUBSCRIBERS NAMES.

G

Duke of Grafton, 10 *copies*
Lord Grosvenor * †
Sir Sampson Gideon, bart. M. P.
Lady Glynne, Howardin-Castle, Flintshire
Lieutenant-General the Hon. T. Gage
Major John Randolph Grymes, late of Virginia.
Mr. Charles Greatrex, Manchester
Mr. Robert Gee, Stockport
Mr. William Greaves, Bakewell

H

Earl of Hillsborough *
Lord Viscount Howe, First Lord of the Admiralty, &c. &c. *
Lieutenant-General the Hon. Sir William Howe, K. B. &c.
Hon. Major-General Harcourt *
Commodore William Hotham, of the Royal Navy
Colonel Hill, late of the 9th. Reg. of Foot
Capt. David Howell, 15th Reg. Dragoons, M.P.
Mr. Hopkins
Ensign Hewgill, Coldstream Guard
Mr. Michael Harris, Millbank-row, Westminster
Mr. —— Hairs, Oxford-street †
Mr. Thomas Hall, Macclesfield
Mr. John Hadfield, ditto
Mr. Micha Hall, Castleton

I

William Jones, esq.
T. I. 3 *copies*

SUBSCRIBERS NAMES.

K

Mr. Thomas Kerſhaw, Derbyſhire
Mr. Kerſley, late of Philadelphia †
Mr. Daniel Key, Uancheſter
Mr. Benjamin Kirk, Brough
Mr. Charles Kirk, Newſmithy

L

Lieutenant General Liſter
Edward Beacher Le Croft, eſq. †
Mr. P. Leyburn, late of Maryland
Mr. Charles Lees, Derbyſhire
B. L.

M

Duke of Montague *
Major-General Martin, Coldſtream Reg. Guards
Colonel Montreſor, late Chief Engineer in America *
Lieutenant Colonel Morſhead
Mr. Iſaac Martin, Bradwell
Mr. Samuel Miller, Bridgehay
Mr. Maſon, Mattock Bath
Mr. Richard Mangnell, Sheffield

N

Lord North *
Lord Newhaven
Mrs. Needham, Perryfoot
Mr. Robert Needham, jun. ditto

O

Sir George Oſborn, bart. M. P. Major General in the Army, Lieutenant-Colonel of the 3d Reg. Foot-Guards, Groom of his Majeſty's Bedchamber, &c.

SUBSCRIBERS NAMES.

Mr. Thomas Oyell, Chappel in Frith.
Mr. Oppie, Great Queen-street, Lincoln's-inn-fields
Mr. Oliphant, Fludyer-street, Westminster * †

P

Duke of Portland *
Lord Viscount Palmerston *
Samuel Phipps, esq. Lincoln's-inn, 2 copies
———— Pollock, esq. * †
Richard Phillips, esq. Lincoln's-inn
Mrs. Charlotte Pringle, Royal Row, Lambeth
Mr. Richard Potter, Derbyshire
Mr. Robert Poole, Button Hill
R. P. 12 copies

Q

R. Quarme, esq.

R

Duke of Richmond
George Rose, esq.
John Randolph, esq. late Attorney General of Virginia
Samuel Remnant, esq.
Mr. Rush, Surgeon of the 2d. Troop of Horse Grenadier Guards
Mr. John Richardson, Derbyshire
Mr. John Robinson, Haslop.

S

Earl of Salisbury *
Lord Viscount Stormont, 4 copies
Lord Viscount Sackville *
Lord Southampton, 2 copies

Sir

SUBSCRIBERS NAMES.

Sir Richard Sutton, bart. M. P. *
Colonel Stevens, 1ft. Reg. Foot Guards, Equerry to the Prince of Wales, and Aid de Camp to the King, &c.
Colonel Sherriff, Portland Place *
Governor Sinnott, of Niagara in Canada
Major Stockton, late of New-Jerfey
Mr. G. S.
Mifs Stopford, Stockport
Mr. John Smith, Manchefter
J. F. S. 7 *copies*

T

Major General H. Trelawny, 1ft Major of the Coldftream Reg. Guards
Mr. Richard Threfher, Strand
Mr. John Thomas, Dean-ftreet, Soho

V

Lieutenant General Vernon, Lieutenant Governor of the Tower

W

Lord Weftcote *
Sir John Borlafe Warren, bart. M. P. &c.
J. Wilmot, efq. M. P. 2 *copies*
Thomas White, efq. Lincoln's-Inn
Eardly Wilmot, efq.
Enfign Webb, Coldftream Reg. Guards
Mr. James Wright, Heafield

Z

W. Z. 5 *copies*

ADVERTISEMENT.

THE late great and very extraordinary revolution in America, a revolution with its attending circumstances unparalleled in the annals of history, having excited the curiosity of all ranks of people, not only of Great Britain, but of every nation in Europe, to procure the most authentic information concerning that country, and there being nothing of the kind hitherto published that gives any satisfactory account thereof, is the cause of my offering these volumes to the public.

The most painful task to me throughout this work has been to mention the hardships

ADVERTISEMENT.

ships and severities I have undergone, as these are now at an end, and freely forgiven; for although I may have much to lament, I solemnly declare that I have no resentments to indulge, no revenge to pursue; and the few instances I met with of kind and generous treatment have afforded me infinite gratification and pleasure to relate.

Far be it from me to wish to widen a breach already too much extended; but those illiberal and vindictive principles which hitherto appear to have actuated the public as well as private conduct of the present prevailing party in America, seem ill calculated for that conciliation which it is certainly still more the interest of America than of Great Britain to effect and cherish.

As the sword of war is now returned to the scabbard, and the beneficial arts of peace may be safely and advantageously cultivated, it would afford infinite satisfaction

ADVERTISEMENT. iii.

faction and pleafure to every benevolent mind to fee, between thefe new American republics, and Great Britain their parent ftate, a contention in good offices, liberal conduct, and generofity, and in fhewing fubftantial proofs on both fides of having buried in oblivion all their former animofities and diftrufts. It is evidently more in the power of the Americans than of the Britifh nation, to evince this conciliatory difpofition, by the lenient conduct they may hereafter adopt towards Britain's former and now forfaken friends, the American loyalifts, whom peculiar circumftances may leave or throw into their power.

Why may not this defirable emulation be excited and adopted? The demon of difcord cannot always influence, nor will the veil of factious refentments and partyfpirit, it is to be hoped, long remain over the fight and underftanding of even the moft zealous of the republicans; they generally poffefs intelligent minds, and confequently

ADVERTISEMENT.

sequently must soon discover and pursue their own interest, which, beyond all doubt, is a close, established, and permanent connection with Great Britain; but it must be a connection founded on confidence, and the basis of that confidence must be a reciprocal interest, urbanity, and friendship.

ERRATA TO VOL. I.

Page 22, line 22, *for* excurfion, *read* exertion. P. 29, l. 10, *dele* been. P. 31, l. 18, *for* ferviſeable, *r.* ſerviceable. P. 33, l. 3, *r.* a thouſand pounds weight. P. 36, L. 15, *r.* expanſes. P. 41, l. 7, *for* excurfion, *r.* exertion. P. 75, l. 21, *dele* upon. P. 78, l. 14, *r.* people's. P. 110, l. 7, *r.* continues. P. 118, l. 11, *for* or, *r.* and. P. 129, *for* Chap. XVI. *r.* XVII. P. 129, l. 5 of the contents, *for* Another ſingular trick, *r.* An extraordinary occurrence. P. 129, l. 18, *for* rather, *r.* ſomewhat. P. 131, l. 9, *dele* with. P. 132. l. 21, *r.* high fun. P. 140, l. 11, *for* experienced, *r.* dextrous. P. 145, l. 15, *r.* within a narrower. P. 155, ſtanza iii. l. 3. *for* the poor, *r.* though poor. P. 159, l. 5. *for* from, *r.* form. P. 173, l. 5, *r.* the men. P. 182, l. 6, *r.* a variety. P. 199, l. 3, *r.* prepoſſeſſed. P. 211. L. 15, *r* reſidence. P. 215, L. 28, *for* ſect, *r.* ſex. P. 290, l. 16, *r.* as all the reſt of their. P. 293, l. 3, *dele* the, *r.* each buſhel. P. 306, l. 6, *for* paſs, *r.* paſſes. P. 319, l. 16, *r.* Ouaſiotto. P. 335, l. 20, 21, 22, 23, *r.* when the incloſure is formed, theſe rails are laid zig zag upon each other, every one croſſing the other obliquely at each end, in regular ſucceſſion and erection, for ten or eleven. P. 347, l. 16, *r.* Kaſquaſquias. P. 349, l. 13, 20, 21, *r.* Ouiſconſins, Puada. P. 373, *l.* 19, *for* land, *r.* load.

CONTENTS.

INTRODUCTION.

The Author's Apology. Acknowledgement of Deficiences. Reasons that induced him to publish these Volumes. Similies. Solicits for Indulgence and Candor. Professes Impartiality and Diffidence. - - - Page 1

CHAP. I.

First Appearance of Land. Capes of Virginia. Chesapeak-Bay. Hampton-Roads. Musketoes. Norfolk. James-River. James-Town. Plantations. Williamsburg - - - - - 7

CHAP. II.

Williamsburg. Races. Breed of Running Horses. 17

CHAP. III.

The different beautiful Situations, and Gentlemen's Seats, on James-River. - - - - - 24

CHAP. IV.

Richmond. Falls of James-River, &c. - 30

CHAP. V.

Inhabitants. Climate. Sky. Thunder and Lightning. Face of the Country. Bullfrogs. Strange and tremendous Sounds. Inchantment. Negroes. 35

VOL. I.   a   CHAP.

CONTENTS.

CHAP. VI.
Manner of Life of each Rank of the Inhabitants. Hard Fare and severe Treatment of the Negroes. Page 41

CHAP. VII.
Houses. Ordinaries, or Inns. A strange Animal. Black Snakes. Devour Frogs and Mice. Fascinate Birds in the Air. Flying Squirrels, &c. - - 49

CHAP. VIII.
Quality and Appearance of the Soil. Wheat. Indian-Corn. Tobacco. Petersburg. Falls of Appamattox. Blandford. Pokahuntas. Indian Emperor's Daughter. Randolph and Bolling Families. The River Appamattox. - - - - 57

CHAP. IX.
General Character, and great Hospitality of the Virginians. Number of Inhabitants in Virginia. - - 65

CHAP. X.
A wretched Situation. Nottoway-River. Horses refuse to eat Bacon. Troublesome Companion. Maherren-River. - - - - - - - 73

CHAP. XI.
North Carolina. Halifax-Town. Roanoak-River. Falls. Rock Fight. Floods. - - - 84

CHAP. XII.
Lofty Timber. Method of clearing Land. Woods on Fire. Dreadful Conflagrations. - - 92

CHAP. XIII.
Inhabitants of the Country and of the Towns. Classes of People. Stores. Planters. Methods of Trade and Commerce. - - - 98

Tarlurg.

CONTENTS.

CHAP. XIV.

Tarburg. Attacked by an itinerant New-light Preacher. Get Lost. Strange Ignorance and uncouth Appearance of the Inhabitants. Instance of extraordinary Hospitality and Benevolence. Chowan Sound. Moccoson Snakes. Rattle Snakes. Cure for their Bite. Page 101

CHAP. XV.

Extraordinary Woman. American General an Innkeeper. Dreadful Thunder-clap. Simplicity of the Negroes. An extraordinary Instance thereof. - - 111

CHAP. XVI.

Nutbush Creek. Member of Congress. Anecdotes of the famous Henderson, and the Origin of the new Settlement of Kentucky. - - - - 122

CHAP. XVII.

Harrisburg. Tar-River. Taken Sick. Extremely ill. Uncivilized Inhabitants. Handsome Women. Instances of worse than savage Brutality. A very singular and diverting Trick. Meet with a beautiful Girl. An extraordinary Occurrence. - 129

CHAP. XVIII.

Woods, Glades, or Savannahs. Licks. Hunters. Wild Horses. Peculiar Sentiments of an European, on his Arrival in America. - - 140

CHAP. XIX.

Appearance of the Country. Diseases of the Climate. Snakes. Game. Raccoons. Description of the Opposum. Beer made of Persimmons. Cheapness of Land. Delightful Climate. Stanzas written in Solitude. 147

CONTENTS.

CHAP. XX.
Newſe-River. Hillſborough. Strong Poſt. Haw Fields. Singular Phenomenon. Accounted for. - Page 159

CHAP. XXI.
Haw-River. Deep-River. Cape Fear River. Carroway Mountains. Grand and elegant Perſpective. Bad Accommodations. Unſuitable to an Epicure, or a Petit-Maitre. - - - - 167

CHAP. XXII.
Yadkin-River. Saliſbury. Beautiful Perſpective. Tryon Mountain. Bruſhy Mountains. The King Mountain diſtinguiſhed for the unhappy Fate of the gallant Major Ferguſon. - - - - - - 174

CHAP. XXIII.
Blazed Path. Origin and Uſe thereof. Deſcription of a Back Wood's Rifleman. His ſtrange Dreſs and peculiar Sentiments. - - - - - 178

CHAP. XXIV.
Catawba Indians. The King. Once a powerful Nation. Cuſtoms. Depopulation. Cauſes thereof. Manner of Life. Abortions of the young Women. - 184

CHAP. XXV.
Catawba's vaſt Property. Their Manufactures. Their Naſtineſs. - - - 192

CHAP. XXVI.
Catawba-River. An uncommon Inſtance of Penury. Rich Miſer. Wretchedneſs and Miſery of his Slaves. Wateree-River. Congarees-River. Santee-River. Their great Extent. Fertility of the Soil. - 196

CHAP.

CONTENTS.

CHAP. XXVII.
Camden. Lands. Rivers. Insects. Inhabitants. Rice. Indigo. Manure. - - Page 202

CHAP. XXVIII.
Great Curiosity of the lower Class of Inhabitants. Impertinent Questions. Conjectures of my Guide. Rendered serviceable. - - - 209

CHAP. XXIX.
Salisbury. Moravian River. Moravian Towns and Settlement. Salem. Bethania. Bethabara. Their Situations. Flourishing State. Their Manufactures. Produce. Peculiar Customs and Police. Women in common - - - - - 213

CHAP. XXX.
The Ararat Mountains. Tryon Mountains. Moravian Mountains. Carraway Mountains. Grand and beautiful perspective Views. - - - - 219

CHAP. XXXI.
Great Allamance. Regulators. Hillsborough. Colonel Mac Donald, and the unfortunate Loyalists of North Carolina. Their Disaster at More's Creek Bridge. Their hard Fate and barbarous Treatment. - 225

CHAP. XXXII.
Hillsborough. Courts of Judicature. Numbers of Inhabitants in North Carolina. Depopulation. Bewildered and lost. Uninhabited Forest. Wild Beasts. Great Danger. Hycoc Creek. Country-Line Creek. 234

CHAP. XXXIII.
Mr. Hart. A most hospitable, benevolent Person. An accomplished Gentleman. Agreeable Surprise. Fortunate

CONTENTS.

tunate Escape. Mr. Bailey. Strange Manner of Lodging. A lovely Girl. Sawra Towns. Sawra Nation. Upper Sawra Towns.   Page 245

CHAP. XXXIV.

Dan-River. Strange and singular Phenomenon. Great Extent. Lower Sawra Towns. A vast and profitable Purchase. Horn, or Hoop Snake. Most poisonous. Alarming Accounts of the Indians. - - 255

CHAP. XXXV.

Ford the Dan. Fall in. Part with my lovely Guide. Get lost. Perplexing Situation. Come upon a Number of Indians. Their Behaviour. Their Hospitality and Kindness. - - - - - 267

CHAP. XXXVI.

Directed the Way by the Indians. Leatherwood Creek. Plantations abandoned. Beaver Creek. Arrive at the Fort. Refused Admittance. - 274

CHAP. XXXVII.

Threaten to set Fire to the Fort. Admitted. Shocking Scenes of Iniquity and Obsceneness within. Ride out and visit the Plantations around. Resolve to set out on my Journey. - - - - 280

CHAP. XXXVIII.

Situation of the Fort. Smith's River. Soil. Ginseng. Snake-root. Prices of Wheat, Corn, Beef, Pork, Tobacco, &c. Culture of Indian Corn. Its great and universal Utility. - - - 288

CHAP. XXXIX.

Set out for Kentucky. Visit the Summit of the Wart Mountain. Description of a most extensive, grand, and elegant Perspective. Ideas raised in the Mind. 300

Descend

CONTENTS.

CHAP. XL.

Defcend the Mountain. Crofs the New River. Middle Fork of Holfton. Arrive at Stahlmakers. Crofs the North Branch of Holfton. Crofs Clinches-River. Afcend the great Allegany. - Page 309

CHAP. XLI.

Crofs the vaft Allegany Mountains. Fall upon the Warrior's Branch. Crofs the Oufiotto Mountains. Impenetrable Thickets of Laurel. River of Kentucky. Arrive at the famed new Settlement on Kentucky. 319

CHAP. XLII.

The famed Settlement of Kentucky. Mr. Henderfon no military Man. Injudicious Forts. A fine commanding Situation. Want of Subordination in America. Hardy Race, but illiberal. Elephants Bones on the Ohio. - - - 326

CHAP. XLIII.

The Rivers Kentucky and Ohio. Woods and Inclofures. Game. Wild Beafts and Fifh. A general Account of the Indians. Their Character. Difpofitions and Numbers. - - - 334

CHAP. XLIV.

A Lift of the Names of all the different Indian Nations on the Continent of North America, with their Situations, and the Number of Gun-men or Warriors in each Nation. - - - 347

CHAP. XLV.

Leave Kentucky. Sail down the Ohio. The Falls of the Ohio. Agreeable Companions. Enter the Miffiffippi, and proceed down that River. Meet fome Chickefaws.

Their

CONTENTS.

Their fine Horses. A gallant Nation. Attacked by a vast Superiority of French and Indians. Defeat them. Their Origin. Their Coavalry. - Page 353

CHAP. XLVI.
Leave Yassous. Arrive at Natches. Proceed to New Orleans. French Inhabitants averse to Spanish Government. Insurrection quelled. Earnestly wish for British Liberty. Number of Families in New Orleans and Louisiana. - - - 365

CHAP. XLVII.
Dangerous Alligators. Vast Fertility of the Soil. Spanish Beards. Wait on the Governor. New Orleans. Great Distresses of some English and French imprisoned by the Spaniards in New Mexico. Vast Flocks of Cattle and Horses. Extensive Savannahs. A good Priest. Leave New Orleans. Arrive at Manchac. Coast along the Gulf of Mexico. Mobile, Pensacola, Apalachichola, &c. - - - - 371

CHAP. XLVIII.
The Rivers Mississippi, Missouris, Illinois, Yassous, Akansas, Rouge, Apalachichola, Mobile, &c. Colorado. North-River, or Rio Bravo. New Mexico. Gulf of California. Mines of Potosi. Acapulco. Old Mexico. La Vera Cruz. Distances of Places. Description of the Country. - - - 385

INTRODUCTION.

The Author's Apology. Acknowledgement of Deficiences. Reasons that induced him to publish these Volumes. Similies. Solicits for Indulgence and Candor. Professes Impartiality and Diffidence.

THE author of the following sheets has no apology or excuse to offer for their publication, but sincerely good intentions, to which, however, he may justly lay claim; and an earnest desire of communicating, and transfusing throughout this the parent state of British America, a more general as well as a more particular knowledge of that extensive and extraordinary country, than seems to prevail at this interesting period, notwithstanding the great, though lately much to be lamented hostile intercourse between that vast continent and these kingdoms,

He

He candidly acknowledges a multitude of deficiences, originating in want of abilities. They are written without ornament or elegance, perhaps in some respects not perfectly accurate, being composed under peculiarly disadvantageous circumstances; but although the subject, as well as the matter, be entirely new, yet he has strictly adhered to truth, which has been his invariable guide and director.

Having very lately arrived in England from America, where he had made many extensive journies, and fatiguing, perilous expeditions, prompted by unbounded curiosity, and an insatiable enthusiastic desire of knowledge, during a residence in that country for a considerable length of time, in which he had become perfectly reconciled and habituated to the manners, customs, dispositions, and sentiments of the inhabitants, he eagerly sought out, and pursued with a degree of avidity rarely felt, every treatise and publication relative to America, from the first discovery by the immortal Columbus,
down

INTRODUCTION.

down to Carver's late Travels therein, and even the Penfilvania Farmer's Letters, by Mr. Hector St. John (if indeed such a person ever exifted); but always had the extreme mortification to meet with difappointment in his expectations, every one grafping at, and enlarging on the greater objects, and not a fingle author defcending to the minutiæ, which compofe as well the true perfpective, as the real grand intercourfe and commerce of life.

Actuated by thefe motives, he was induced to hazard this undertaking, wifhing to fupply that neceffary fhare of inferior knowledge, which to him appeared to be wanting in Great Britain, the original feat of empire, from the deficiences already pointed out.

For a defcription of the formation of a fingle brick, of a vaft multitude of which, artfully arranged, prodigious buildings and elegant palaces are conftructed, to a perfon entirely unacquainted with fuch a thing, is as neceffary, beneficial, and fometimes equally agreeable as the defcription of the edifice itfelf.

And the particular mode in forming the compofition for making the fineft china is more fought after, and certainly of no lefs value, than the moft elegant, rich, and expenfive fet of porcelain of the beft Drefden manufacture.

In one refpect he folicits the indulgence of the public. As feveral matters related in the courfe of the following pages are perfectly novel, uncommon, and ftrange to an European reader, efpecially to a Briton, who may thereby be induced to decide againft the veracity and probability of the whole, from the apparent incredibility, to him, of fuch fingular phenomena, and in his opinion, marvellous, furprifing relations; on thefe occafions, he entreats the man of candour only to fufpend his cenfure and judgment, in fuch inftances, either until he meets with fome intelligent perfon in whom he can confide, and on whofe decifion he may rely, who has made a confiderable refidence in, and progrefs through that extraordinary country; or until he communicates

INTRODUCTION.

municates his doubts and difficulties through the channel of the public, and ballances in his mind the weight of the explanation and defence he may obferve in reply, fupported by fuch authority as may be adduced.

For however fingular, wonderful, and aftonifhing fome things herein may appear, yet the author folemnly declares he has been guided folely by nature and truth, which, during the courfe of his life, as well as in this relation, he has always endeavored to purfue, and to pay implicit obedience to their venerable dictates.

On this principle alone he has attempted to folve every difficulty that occurred to him in his travels; and fuch uncommon appearances, and ftrange phenomena, as to fome have feemed not to be eafily accounted for, he has always found more reconcilable to, and confiftent with, the plain and fimple chain of events, regularly proceeding from natural caufes, than the imaginary fplendid embel-

embellishments of fiction, however ingenious and elegant.

Should these Volumes be favorably received, and deemed to merit the notice and approbation of the public, he means to proceed with a brief account of the late war, in regular progression, from its commencement down to the present period. If otherwise, he conceives the publication of two volumes void of desert, is a sufficient obtrusion on the public, to whom, as well as to himself, it will be most agreeable, and more discreet, to cancel or suppress the remainder.

However, he trusts that a proper distinction will be made between his capacity and his good intentions, flattering himself, that what is wanting in the former may be supplied by the latter; and will endeavour to atone for his deficiences in abilities, by the strictest candour and impartiality.

On these grounds, therefore, he rests his expectations, and awaits the decision.

A TOUR
IN THE
UNITED STATES OF AMERICA.

CHAP. I.

First Appearance of Land. Capes of Virginia. Chesapeak-Bay. Hampton-Roads. Musketoes. Norfolk. James-River. James-Town. Plantations. Williamsburg.

WE came in sight of land, on the fourth day of August, in the forenoon, in a fine day, with a clear serene sky. It appeared at a distance like the tops of the trees just emerging above the horizon, on the surface of the water; and as the ship approached arose higher, but only the height of the pines, with which all the land on the sea board is covered; for the whole coast is very low, and soundings are found at a great distance from the shore, which gradually decrease as you advance nearer the land.

This regular decrease of the soundings, and the change of colour in the water, are the only preservatives of ships, in the night and hazy weather, from running on this dangerous, shallow, flat coast, without perceiving it until too late; for there is no light-house near the Capes of Virginia: a most laudable intention of erecting one on Cape Charles having been frustrated by a disagreement between the assemblies or parliaments of Virginia and Maryland, at whose joint expence it was to have been built and supported; and by the commencement of the late inauspicious hostilities in America.

We soon sailed within the Capes of Virginia, Cape Henry and Cape Charles, which last is an island named Smith's.

We paſt Lynhaven Bay on our left, and the opening of the Cheſapeak on the right, and in the evening anchored in Hampton Road, which appears to be very ſafe.

The diſtance between the Capes is about twelve miles, but the vaſt bay of Cheſapeak widens after you enter, until it becomes about thirty miles over, near thirty-five Engliſh leagues within land; then the breadth decreaſes from thence to the head of it, and is generally from fifteen to five miles, which is the breadth of it at its extremity, where the Elk and the mighty river Suſquahannah fall into it, at about three hundred miles diſtance from the ſea, through the whole of which vaſt extent the tide ebbs and flows.

The night being calm we were aſſaulted by great numbers of muſketoes, a very noxious fly, which ſeems to be of the ſpecies of gnats, but larger and more poiſonous, leaving a hard tumor wherever they bite, with an intolerable and painful itching; they penetrate the ſkin, fill themſelves with blood, and make their

principal

principal attacks in the night, accompanied by a small, shrill, disagreeable note, the very sound of which effectually prevents you from sleep, after you have been once bit.

On the day following, the captain of the ship, Mr. R———, and I went up Elizabeth River, in the yaul, to Norfolk, about twenty miles, where we dined very agreeably, and returned that evening to the ship in Hampton Road, so that I had not at this time an opportunity of seeing much of the town. However, it appears to be charmingly situated at the forks of a very pleasant river, the Elizabeth, on the north-east side, Mr. Sprowle's little village of Gosport being on the south, and the pretty town of Portsmouth on the south-west side, over against Norfolk, at the distance of about eight hundred yards, which is the breadth of the river there; with sufficient depth of water for a ship of the line.

Norfolk is a corporation, with a mayor, aldermen, &c. in a flourishing state of im-

improvement, and increasing daily; it contains about seven thousand inhabitants, of all colours and denominations, of which perhaps more than two thousand are whites. But it was by no means in such a state of increase and improvement as the more inland towns, at or near the falls of the great rivers; these being the chief emporiums of trade and commerce for the large, populous, and extensive back country, west and south of them; and, having also all the advantages of navigation, intercept the inland trade from Norfolk, which renders it, though flourishing, yet only so in an inferior degree.

[Soon after the commencement of the late unhappy and ill-fated hostilities in America, the beautiful town of Norfolk fell a sacrifice to the mistaken fury and devastations of civil war; in an unfortunate measure of the British governor of Virginia, rendered excusable however, and even very justifiable, by the circumstances

stances attending it; and the more imprudent, criminal, and even vindictive, savage depredations of a back-wood's mob of American soldiery, who seemed then to carry their unjust, barbarous, and ill-grounded resentments against all the low-country and sea-coast; having proposed even to spread desolation throughout the whole, merely because it was within reach and command of the British navy; and because the principles and conduct of the inhabitants were more temperate and liberal than theirs.

The American soldiery, chiefly then back-woods riflemen, taking every opportunity of firing from under the cover of the houses and wharfs, upon the British troops, and loyalists who had been compelled to seek refuge on board the shipping then in the river, by this means picking off a few individuals every day, in this sneaking, cowardly manner; a message was sent them by his majesty's governor, the earl of Dunmore, who was then on board the fleet, requesting them
to

to defift from fuch unjuftifiable practices, otherwife he fhould be compelled to fire upon the town, perhaps to its deftruction, though very reluctantly: but they perfifting in their defpicable unmilitary offences, he fent them orders to remove all the women and children out of the place by a limited time, when a cannonade would certainly be commenced upon the town; and the fhips of war were drawn near, and prepared for that purpofe. This being accordingly executed, and the enemy galling the troops from the warehoufes on the wharfs, thefe were obliged to be fet on fire to diflodge them, which was thus completely effected; but it was univerfally noticed, and particularly obferved by every perfon, that almoft at the fame inftant the flames broke out likewife in the back part of the town, fartheft from the fhipping; for the rebels had alfo fet fire to it, in many different places themfelves, by order of the provincial congrefs of Virginia, by which means the conflagration foon became general and tremendous, and in a fhort time entirely

tirely deftroyed, and confumed to afhes this fine town, the firft in Virginia in magnitude, opulence, and navigation.

The Americans not only burnt Norfolk, but the village of Gofport, and a great part of the beautiful little town of Portfmouth alfo, fince that time; and, by an act of their legiflature, granted a compenfation in money to fuch perfons as were well affected to their caufe, for the value of their property thus deftroyed.]

On the fixth, the fhip weighed anchor, and proceeded up James River. As the weather was extremely hot, I preferred going up in her to a journey by land; which, from Norfolk to Richmond, at the falls of James River, is about an hundred and thirty miles.

After paffing a great number of moft charming fituations on each fide of this beautiful river, we came to anchor before James Town, now a paltry place, not by any means deferving even the name of
a vil-

a village, although once the metropolis of Virginia, and still possessing several privileges in consequence thereof, one of which is sending a member to the assembly, or parliament; who is now Champion Traverse, esq. the proprietor of the whole town, and almost all the land adjacent, and I believe there are no more voters than himself.

On the seventh, Mr. R—— and I, having been furnished with horses by Mr. Traverse, made an excursion to Williamsburg, which is but a few miles distant; perhaps eight or ten.

The roads are excellent, the face of the country is level, the soil rather sandy, but the whole land appears to be one continued immense forest, interspersed with openings where the trees have been cut down, and the ground is cultivated, of larger or less dimensions: these are called plantations, and are generally from one to four or five miles distant from each other, having a dwelling-house in the middle, with kitchens and out-houses all

detached

detached; at fome little diftance there are always large peach and apple orchards, &c.; and fcattered over the plantations are the tobacco houfes, large wooden edifices, for the cure of that grand ftaple produce.

We dined very agreeably at the Raleigh tavern, where we had exceeding good Madeira, and afterwards walked out to view the town, which is now the feat of government, and metropolis of Virginia.

CHAP.

CHAP. II.

Williamsburg. Races. Breed of Running-Horses.

WILLIAMSBURG is an inland town on the higheſt land about the middle between the rivers of York, on the north, and James, on the ſouth, at the diſtance of ſeven miles from the neareſt; and is healthy for the climate.

There is one handſome ſtreet in it, juſt a mile in length, where the view is terminated by a commanding object each way; the Capitol, an elegant public building, in which the aſſembly, or ſenate, and courts of judicature are held, at one end of the ſtreet; and the college of William and Mary, an old monaſtic ſtructure, at the other end. About the middle between them, on the north ſide, a little diſtance retired from the ſtreet, ſtands the palace, the reſidence of the governor;

a large, commodious, and handsome building.

[Since the commencement of the late hoſtilities in America, when the ſeat of war was in Virginia, about the time of, or ſoon after lord Cornwallis's ſurrender at York Town, the Americans converted the palace at Williamſburg into barracks for the accommodation of their troops; who, being by no means remarkable for cleanneſs or care, by ſome accident ſet it on fire, by which it was entirely deſtroyed; thus occaſioned, as many imagine, by their neglect. It has alſo been alledged, that ſome loyaliſts, provoked at ſeeing it converted to ſuch vile purpoſes, ſo very different from the original intention of the ſtructure; and incenſed in the higheſt degree at beholding the houſe of the repreſentative of their ſovereign thus polluted by the naſtineſs, filth, and depredations of the American ſoldiery, privately ſet fire to it in the night: and they are

are not few who believe that to this laſt cauſe it owed its ruin.]

All the public edifices are built of brick, but the generality of the houſes are of wood, chiefly painted white, and are every one detached from each other; which, with the ſtreet deep with ſand, (not being paved) makes a ſingular appearance to an European; and is very diſagreeable to walk in, eſpecially in ſummer, when the rays of the ſun are intenſely hot, and not a little increaſed by the reflection of the white ſand, wherein every ſtep is almoſt above the ſhoe, and where there is no ſhade or ſhelter to walk under, unleſs you carry an umbrella.

There is a whimſical circumſtance attends Williamſburg; which is, a part of the town (that has been added to it ſince it was firſt built) having the ſtreets laid out in the form of a W.

Williamſburg is alſo the county-town of James-city county; where the courts of common pleas are held monthly, as they

they are also in every county in the colony; which amount to sixty-eight in number. The quarter sessions are also held quarterly in each county. Besides these, there are two courts of oyer and terminer held annually at Williamsburg; and likewise two general courts in April and October, which receive and determine appeals from every county, and all the inferior courts, as well as try original causes for sums above twenty pounds.

These, as also the courts of chancery, courts of admiralty, and assemblies or parliaments, besides the college, occasion a great resort and concourse of people to Williamsburg; and are indeed the chief, if not the whole, support of the place: for her share of commerce is very inconsiderable, and she does not possess a single manufacture.

There are races at Williamsburg twice a year; that is, every spring and fall, or autumn. Adjoining to the town is a very excellent course, for either two, three or four mile heats. Their purses are generally gerally raifed by fubfcription, and are gained by the horfe that wins two four-mile heats out of three; they amount to an hundred pounds each for the firft day's running, and fifty pounds each every day after; the races commonly continuing for a week. There are alfo matches and fweepftakes very often, for confiderable fums. Befides thefe at Williamfburg, there are races eftablifhed annually, almoft at every town and confiderable place in Virginia; and frequent matches, on which large fums of money depend; the inhabitants, almoft to a man, being quite devoted to the diverfion of horfe-racing.

Very capital horfes are ftarted here, fuch as would make no defpicable figure at Newmarket; nor is their fpeed, bottom, or blood inferior to their appearance; the gentlemen of Virginia fparing no pains, trouble, or expence in importing the beft ftock, and improving the excellence of the breed by proper and judicious croffing.

Indeed nothing can be more elegant and beautiful than the horses bred here, either for the turf, the field, the road, or the coach; and they have always fine long, full, flowing tails; but their carriage horses seldom are possessed of that weight and power, which distinguish those of the same kind in England.

Their stock is from old Cade, old Crab, old Partner, Regulus, Babraham, Bosphorus, Devonshire Childers, the Cullen Arabian, the Cumberland Arabian, &c. in England; and a horse from Arabia, named the Bellsize, which was imported into America, and is now in existence.

'In the southern part of the colony, and in North Carolina, they are much attached to *quarter-racing*, which is always a match between two horses, to run one quarter of a mile streight out; being merely an excursion of speed; and they have a breed that perform it with astonishing velocity, beating every other, for that distance, with great ease; but they have no bottom. However, I am confident
that

that there is not a horſe in England, nor perhaps the whole world, that can excel them in rapid ſpeed: and theſe likewiſe make excellent ſaddle horſes for the road.

The Virginians, of all ranks and denominations, are exceſſively fond of horſes, and eſpecially thoſe of the race breed. The gentlemen of fortune expend great ſums on their ſtuds, generally keeping handſome carriages, and ſeveral elegant ſets of horſes, as well as others for the race and road: even the moſt indigent perſon has his ſaddle-horſe, which he rides to every place, and on every occaſion; for in this country nobody walks on foot the ſmalleſt diſtance, except when hunting: indeed a man will frequently go five miles to catch a horſe, to ride only one mile upon afterwards. In ſhort, their horſes are their pleaſure, and their pride.

CHAP. III.

The different beautiful Situations, and Gentlemen's Seats, on James River.

IN the evening, Mr. R—— and I were unfortunately separated, occasioned by a very ridiculous and singular accident; the effect of which had like to have been tragical enough to him. Just when we were ready to return to the ship, by some mistake, wrong horses were brought to the door; and not observing it, we mounted them: these horses being very spirited, and Mr. R——, having bid adieu to the gentlemen with whom we dined, suddenly clapped both his spurs in his horse's sides, inadvertently, with great force; the horse instantly reared up, and sprung forwards, leaving poor R—— upon the ground, at the door, flat on his back, with his skull almost fractured. By this means the mistake in the change of our horses was discovered and rectified; but Mr. R—— was so much hurt, that
he

he was obliged to be blooded, and carried into the Raleigh again, where I left him; and was thereby reduced to the neceſſity of returning alone to the ſhip.

On the ninth of Auguſt the ſhip got under weigh, and proceeded up the river, paſſing the delightful ſituations of Sandy-Point, Cabin-Point, Brandon, Flower de Hundred, Maycox, &c. on the ſouth ſide; and Swine-Yards, belonging to Mr. Cole, Colonel Byrd's beatuiful ſeat of Weſt-over, Colonel Harriſon's of Barclay, &c. on the north ſide: we anchored oppoſite to City-Point, at the confluence of the Appamatox River and the James, and about an hundred and thirty miles within land, from the capes of Virginia.

Here the ſecond mate was carried on ſhore to the houſe of a Mrs. Brown, having been for a conſiderable time languiſhing, and in great pain, occaſioned by a violent contuſion he received by a fall on the deck from the main-yard-arm, reefing the main-ſail in a gale of wind; and ſoon after he ended his days there.

As

As the ship was not to go much farther up, and was to receive great part of her cargo at this place, I hired a boat and four negroes, for one dollar and a half per day (about six shillings and ninepence sterling); and on the tenth I left the ship moored, and proceeded up the river in the boat; proposing to land at every place whose beauty of perspective, or singular appearance of any kind, might strike the attention, or excite my curiosity.

I had almost omitted to mention an unfortunate accident that happened at this place, before I left the ship. A young sailor, having killed and cut up a fine large sturgeon, that had leaped out of the water and fallen into the boat, along side of the ship, which happens frequently here; bringing in the last piece himself, in his hand, his foot slipped off the gunwale of the boat, between which and the ship he fell into the river, and was never seen or heard of more.

The principal situations that commanded my notice and admiration, were
Shirley

Shirley Hundred, a feat of Charles Carter, efq. at prefent in occupation of Mr. Bowler Cock: this is indeed a charming place; the buildings are of brick, large, convenient, and expenfive, but now falling to decay; they were erected at a great charge, by Mr. Carter's father, who was fecretary of the colony, and this was his favourite feat of refidence. The prefent proprietor has a moft opulent fortune, and poffeffes fuch a variety of feats, in fituations fo exceedingly delightful, that he overlooks this fweet one of Shirley, and fuffers it to fall to ruin, although the buildings muft have coft an immenfe fum in conftructing; and would certainly be expenfive to keep in repair, which expence, however, muft be greatly increafed by this neglect.

Varina, the feat of Ryland Randolph, efq. a moft lovely and delightful fpot: an elegant building, but unfiniſhed, occafioned by the owner's verfatility of tafte, and perpetual alterations. .

Chat-

Chatsworth, the seat of William Randolph, esq. whose father was surveyor-general of the southern district of North-America, &c, is a very good house, with an agreeable perspective.

A Mr. Mayho's; a very pretty place also.——All on the north side of the James.

On the south side are the beautiful little towns of Bermuda Hundred, Osborn's, and Warwick: and a seat belonging to a Mr. Cary; a lovely situation, who has also erected some extremely valuable mills, iron-works, &c. of equal emolument and importance to himself and the community. They are situated near the town of Warwick, about five miles below Richmond, and the falls of James-River.

[These valuable mills and iron works have been set fire to, and entirely destroyed, during the late unhappy war, in 1781, in an expedition under the command of Brigadier General Arnold.]

I slept on board the boat; and on the eleventh, in the forenoon, landed at the town of Shokoes, at the falls of James-River, and immediately discharged the boat.

I then waited on Mr. ———, a merchant, at that place, on whom I had been been furnished with letters of credit, &c. He was at home, and received me with kindness, attention, and friendship. He offered me apartments in his house, which I accepted, and he seemed studious to serve and amuse me.

CHAP.

CHAP. IV.

Richmond. Falls of James-River, &c.

AT this place the whole appearance of the country undergoes a total change. From the sea to the falls, about one hundred and fifty-five miles, there is not a hill to be seen; scarcely an eminence, being one continued flat level, without even a single stone to be found; nothing but sand and shells on the shores, and the land consists of loam, sand, and clay, but universally covered with woods.

Here a ledge of rocks interrupts the whole stream of the river, for the length of seven miles; during the course of which, that vast current of water rushes down, raging with impetuosity, tumbling and dashing from rock to rock, with an astonishing roar, that is heard for many miles distance. The land suddenly swells into hills of a great height, and abounds with

with prodigious rocks, and large stones, as well as trees.

On the summits of these hills, most of which over-look, and many of them over-hang the falling torrent of the James, handsome houses are built, which command a wild, grand, and most elegant perspective.

The James, here, is about half a mile wide; the tide flows up to the very rocks of the falls, which continue to interrupt the current for the length of seven miles above. There are several islands in the river among the falls, which are chiefly covered with wood and rocks; but are of small extent: the tide reaches the lower end of one of these islands, which is serviseable in checking the violence of the torrent of the water in the falls, and thereby favours the passage of the ferry boats below.

There are three towns at this place. Richmond, the largest, is below the falls, and is separated only by a creek, named Shokoes, from the town of Shokoes, which
joins

joins the lower end of the falls; these are both on the north side of the river: on the south side stands the town of Chesterfield, best known by the name of Rocky-Ridge, from its situation.

Vessels of small burthen come up to the rocks of the falls, and large ships come within two miles of them to load.

At James town, the river is between two and three miles wide; and just above it is always fresh water: the breadth decreases gradually to the falls.

During my residence at Richmond, I made several little excursions around in the adjacent country, on visits to several gentlemen, who honoured me with invitations. Among those, from whom I received particular attention and civilities, were Thomas Mann Randolph, of Tuckahoe, esq. R. Good, of Chesterfield, esq. Mr. Cary, &c.

I also rode as far as Westham, a small town on the James, seven miles above Richmond, just where the falls commence. Tobacco, the grand staple of Virginia, is navigated down the river from the back country to Weftham, in hogfheads of a thoufand weight each, ready for exportation, every hogfhead upon two canoes lafhed together; then it is brought by land-carriage to Shokoes, or Richmond, as the falls totally intercept and preclude all communication by water for their continuance of feven miles.

In floods, an immenfe body of water comes down the James, which fwells to a great height and aftonifhing widenefs, overflowing all the low ground for many miles; but at the falls, where the mountains arife abruptly on each fide, and confine the river within more narrow bounds, the noife, violence, and impetuofity of the torrent, is not to be defcribed. It is dreadfully tremenduous and awful.

It feems that once, when the river was in fuch a ftate, a man, who was bringing down his tobacco to market, inftead of landing at Weftham, being quite intoxicated with fpirituous liquor, was carried down the torrent; and, amazing to think on!

on! arrived safe at Shokoes warehouse-wharf below, with his tobacco; having been brought to the shore, after he had got over all the falls, by boats sent out from thence to his assistance, by those, who with astonishment and horror, observed him in his dreadful rapid descent and passage over them. When he was brought to the shore, he was still in a state of insensibility and stupefaction, occasioned by inebriation and terror.

This is indeed one of the most extraordinary accidents that has occurred, or perhaps was ever heard of; but I have no reason to doubt the fact, as it was related to me, and vouched for, by several persons of credit and veracity, who were eye-witnesses of this singular event.

CHAP.

CHAP. V.

Inhabitants. Climate. Sky. Thunder and Lightning. Face of the Country. Bullfrogs. Strange and tremendous Sounds. Inchantment. Negroes.

THE customs and manner of living of most of the white inhabitants here, I must confess, did not a little surprise me; being inactive, languid, and enervating to the last degree.

Indeed the whole appearance of the country, and face of nature, is strikingly novel and charming to an European, especially to a Briton.

The air, the sky, the water, the land, and the inhabitants, being two-thirds blacks, are objects entirely different from all that he had been accustomed to see before. The sky clear and serene, very seldom over-cast, or any haze to be observed in the atmosphere; the rains falling in torrents, and the clouds immediately dispersing. Frequent dreadful thun-

der in loud contending peals; thunder gufts happening often daily, and always within every two or three days, at this feafon of the year. Erufcations and flafhes of lightning, conftantly fucceeding each other, in quick and rapid traufitions. The air dry, and intenfely hot in the fummer, cold and piercing in the winter, and always keen and penetrating. During the night, thoufands of lights, like bright burning candles, being large winged infects, called fire-flies, gliding through the air in every direction; frequently vanifhing, and perpetually fucceeded by new ones. The rivers, large expances of water, of enormous extent, and fpreading under the eye as far as it can comprize; nature here being on fuch a fcale, that what are called great rivers in Europe, are here confidered only as inconfiderable creeks or rivulets. The land, an immenfe foreft, extended on a flat plain, almoft without bounds; or arifing into abrupt afcents, and at length fwelling into ftupendous mountains, interfperfed with
rocks

rocks and precipices, yet covered with venerable trees, hoary with age, and torn with tempefts. The mountains fuddenly broken through, and fevered by mighty rivers, raging in torrents at the bottom of the tremendous chafm, or gliding in awful majeftic filence along the deep vallies between them. The agriculture on the plantations is different from every thing in Europe; being either tobacco, three feet high, with the plants a yard apart; or Indian corn, at the diftance of fix feet between each ftalk, in regular ftreight rows, or avenues, frequently twelve or fifteen feet in height.

While the mind is filled with aftonifhment, and novel objects, all the fenfes are gratified.

The flowery fhrubs which over-fpread the land, regale the fmell with odoriferous perfumes: and fruits of exquifite relifh and flavour, delight the tafte, and afford a moft grateful refrefhment.

The prodigious multitude of green frogs, reptiles, and large infects, on the trees, as well as the bull-frogs in the swamps, ponds, and places of water, during the spring, summer, and fall, make an inceffant noife and clamour; the bull-frogs, in particular, emitting a moft tremendous roar, louder than the bellowing of a bull, from the fimilarity of whofe voice they obtained their name; but their note is harfh, fonorous, and abrupt, frequently appearing to pronounce articulate founds, in ftriking refemblance to the following words, *Hogfhead tobacco*, *Knee deep*. *Ancle deep*. *Deeper and deeper*. *Piankitank*, and many others; but all equally grating and diffonant. They furprife a man exceedingly, as he will hear their hoarfe, loud, bellowing clamor juft by him, and fometimes all around him, yet he cannot difcover from whence it proceeds; they being all covered in water, and juft raifing their mouth only a little above the furface when they roar out, then inftantly draw it under again. They are of the fize of a man's foot,

United States of America. 39

Nor can you perceive the animals from whence the founds in the trees proceed, they being moſt effectually hid among the leaves and branches. So that at firſt this abſolutely appears to be a country of enchantments.

As I obſerved before, at leaſt two-thirds of the inhabitants are negroes, whoſe difference of features and colour, and rank offenſive ſmell, are extremely diſagreeable and diſguſtful to Europeans: but, poor creatures! they are all humility and ſubmiſſion; and it is the greateſt pleaſure of their lives, when they can pleaſe the whites.

You cannot underſtand all of them, as great numbers, being Africans, are incapable of acquiring our language, and at beſt but very imperfectly, if at all; many of the others alſo ſpeak a mixed dialect between the Guinea and Engliſh.

It is fortunate for humanity, that theſe poor creatures poſſeſs ſuch a fund of contentment and reſignation in their

D 4 minds;

minds; for they indeed seem to be the happiest inhabitants in America, notwithstanding the hardness of their fare, the severity of their labour, and the unkindness, ignominy, and often barbarity of their treatment.

CHAP,

CHAP. VI.

Manner of Life of each Rank of the Inhabitants.

TO give an idea of the manner in which a white man spends his time in this country, a description is necessary of each degree in life.

The gentleman of fortune rises about nine o'clock; he perhaps may make an excursion to walk as far as his stables to see his horses, which is seldom more than fifty yards from his house; he returns to breakfast, between nine and ten, which is generally tea or coffee, bread and butter, and very thin slices of venison-ham, or hung beef. He then lies down on a pallat, on the floor, in the coolest room in the house, in his shirt and trousers only, with a negro at his head, and another at his feet, to fan him, and keep off the flies; between twelve and one he takes a draught of bombo, or toddy, a liquor composed of water, sugar, rum,

and

and nutmeg, which is made weak, and kept cool: he dines between two and three, and at every table, whatever elfe there may be, a ham and greens or cabbage, is always a ftanding difh; at dinner he drinks cyder, toddy, punch, port, claret, and madeira, which is generally excellent here: having drank fome few glaffes of wine after dinner, he returns to his pallat, with his two blacks to fan him, and continues to drink toddy, or fangaree, all the afternoon: he does not always drink tea; between nine and ten in the evening, he eats a light fupper of milk and fruit, or wine, fugar, and fruit, &c. and almoft immediately retires to bed, for the night; in which, if it be not furnifhed with mufketoe curtains, he is generally fo molefted with the heat, and harraffed and tormented with thofe pernicious infects the mufketoes, that he receives very little refrefhment from fleep.

This is his general way of living in his family, when he has no company.

No doubt many differ from it, some in one respect, some in another; but more follow it than do not.

The lower, and many of the middling classes, live very differently. A man in this line rises in the morning about six o'clock; he then drinks a julap, made of rum, water, and sugar, but very strong; then he walks, or more generally rides, round his plantation, views all his stock, and all his crop, breakfasts about ten o'clock, on cold turkey, cold meat, fried homminy, toast and cyder, ham, bread and butter, tea, coffee, or chocolate, which last, however, is seldom tasted but by the women; the rest of the day he spends much in the same manner before described in a man of the first rank, only cyder supplies the place of wine at dinner, and he eats no supper; they never even think of it. The women very seldom drink tea in the afternoon; the men never.

The poor negro slaves alone work hard, and fare still harder. It is astonishing,
and

and unaccountable to conceive what an amazing degree of fatigue thefe poor, but happy, wretches do undergo, and can fupport. He is called up in the morning at day break, and is feldom allowed time enough to fwallow three mouthfuls of homminy, or hoe-cake, but is driven out immediately to the field to hard labour; at which he continues, without intermiffion, until noon; and it is obferved, as a fingular circumftance, that they always carry out a piece of fire with them, and kindle one juft by their work, let the weather be ever fo hot and fultry. About noon is the time he eats his dinner, and he is feldom allowed an hour for that purpofe. His meal confifts of homminy and falt, and, if his mafter be a man of humanity, he has a little fat, fkimmed milk, rufty bacon, or falt herring to relifh his homminy, or hoe-cake, which kind mafters allow their flaves twice a week: but the number of thofe, it is much to be lamented, are very few; for the poor flave generally fares

the

the worfe for his mafter's riches, which confifting of land and negroes, their numbers increafe their hardfhips, and diminifh their value to the proprietor, the expence precluding an extenfion of indulgence and liberality.

They then return to fevere labour, which continues in the field until dufk in the evening, when they repair to the tobacco-houfes, where each has his tafk in ftripping allotted him, that employs him for fome hours. If it be found, next morning, that he has neglected, flighted, or not performed his labour, he is tied up, and receives a number of lafhes, on his bare back, moft feverely inflicted, at the difcretion of thofe unfeeling fons of barbarity, the overfeers, who are permitted to exercife an unlimited dominion over them.

It is late at night before he returns to his fecond fcanty meal, and even the time taken up at it, encroaches upon his hours of fleep, which, altogether, do never exceed

ceed eight in number, for eating and repose.

But instead of retiring to rest, as might naturally be concluded he would be glad to do, he generally sets out from home, and walks six or seven miles in the night, be the weather ever so sultry, to a negroe dance, in which he performs with astonishing agility, and the most vigorous exertions, keeping time and cadence, most exactly, with the music of a banjor (a large hollow instrument with three strings), and a quaqua (somewhat resembling a drum), until he exhausts himself, and scarcely has time, or strength, to return home before the hour he is called forth to toil next morning.

When he sleeps, his comforts are equally miserable and limited; for he lies on a bench, or on the ground, with only an old scanty single blanket, and not always even that, to serve both for his bed and his covering. Nor is his cloathing less niggardly and wretched, being nothing but a shirt and trousers, made of
coarse

coarse thin hard hempen stuff in the summer, with the addition of a sordid woollen jacket, breeches, and shoes, in the winter.

The female slaves fare, labour, and repose, just in the same manner; even when they breed, which is generally every two or three years, they seldom lose more than a week's work thereby, either in the delivery, or suckling the child.

In submission to injury and insults, they are likewise obliged to be entirely passive, nor dare any of them resist, or even defend himself against the whites, if they should attack him without the smallest provocation; for the law directs a negroe's arm to be struck off, who raises it against a white person, should it be only in his own defence, against the most wanton and wicked barbarity and outrage.

Yet notwithstanding this degrading situation, and rigid severity to which fate has subjected this wretched race, they are
certainly

certainly devoid of care, and actually appear jovial, contented, and happy. Fortunate it is indeed for them, that they are blessed with this easy, satisfied disposition of mind, else human nature, unequal to the weight, must sink under the pressure of such complicated misery and wretchedness.

Having had occasion more than once to mention *homminy, hoe-cake, &c,* it may not be improper at this time to observe, that homminy is an American dish, made of Indian corn, freed from the husks, boiled whole, along with a small proportion of a large kind of French beans, until it becomes almost a pulp: it is in general use, and to my taste, very agreeable. Hoe-cake is Indian corn, ground into meal, kneaded into dough, and baked on a hot, broad, iron hoe. This is also in common use, and to my palate, extremely harsh and unpleasant.

CHAP.

CHAP. VII.

Houses. Ordinaries, or Inns. A strange Animal. Black Snakes. Devour Frogs and Mice. Fascinate Birds in the Air. Flying Squirrels, &c.

THE houses here are almost all of wood, covered with the same; the roof with shingles, the sides and ends with thin boards, and not always lathed and plaistered within; only those of the better sort are finished in that manner, and painted on the outside. The chimneys are sometimes of brick, but more commonly of wood, coated on the inside with clay. The windows of the best sort have glass in them; the rest have none, and only wooden shutters.

There is no distinction here between inns, taverns, ordinaries, and public-houses; they are all in one, and are known by the appellation of taverns, public-houses, or ordinaries, which, in the general acceptance of the names here, are synonymous terms. They are all very

very indifferent indeed, compared with the inns in England: and three-fourths of them are in reality little better than mere shelters from the weather; yet the worst of them is by no means deficient in charging high.

When a person arrives at Richmond, his ears are continually assailed with the prodigious noise and roaring of the falls, which almost stuns him, and prevents him from sleeping for several nights, it being a considerable time before he becomes habituated to it.

My principal amusement was walking: I took great delight in wandering alone among the rocks and solitary romantic situations, around the falls. In these excursions I always carried a book in my pocket, and when I came to any place that commanded my attention, either from the wildness and grandeur of the perspective, or from the observation of the raging torrent below, after admiring the beauties of the scene, I would frequently lie down in the shade, and amuse

amuse myself with reading, until I insensibly dropt asleep. This was my daily recreation, which I never neglected.

But I was once extremely surprised at beholding, as soon as I opened my eyes, a prodigious large snake, within a few feet of me, basking himself in the sun. He was jet black, with a copper-coloured belly, very fine sparkling eyes, and at least seven feet long. However he did me no injury; for I did not disturb him, nor did he molest me; but as soon as he heard the rustling of the leaves, on my moving, he went off with great precipitation and speed.

Another time, whilst I was reading in a very solitary retired place among the rocks and trees, on hearing some little noise near me, I looked around, and just had the glimpse of a very strange and singular animal, such as I had never seen even any resemblance of before. It appeared to me more like a fiddle with feet, than any thing else that I know; the sight I had of it was just as it was running behind a rock. I fought there, and every where for it immediately, to no purpofe, for I could not difcover even a trace thereof remaining.

When I returned, I mentioned what I had feen; but no one, from my defcription, could inform me what animal it was*.

However, nothing is more common here than the black fnake. He is very bold and daring; yet, to the human race, entirely harmlefs and inoffenfive; nor is his bite poifonous, and is as readily cured as the fcratch of a briar: notwithftanding which, it is faid, and I believe with truth, that he is mafter of all other fnakes; even the rattle-fnake fubmits to him. This fuperiority arifes from the ftrength and power of his mufcles, for he infinuates himfelf in fpiral wreaths around his antagonift, and then contracting, by that means conquers or kills him. His prey, for food, he fwallows whole.

* For a defcription of this animal, fee chap. xxIII.

It is confidently reported, and univerſally credited, that they devour ſquirrels, and that they have been found with ſquirrels whole in their bellies. I myſelf have ſeen them ſwallow frogs of a very large ſize. After the frog is almoſt wholly in, if you ſtrike the ſnake, he will inſtantly diſgorge it, and the frog will leap away.

The black ſnakes are particularly ſerviceable in deſtroying rats and mice, which they ſeek after very eagerly, and devour for food: for this purpoſe, they are even more uſeful than cats, becauſe, by their ſlender form and peculiar make, they are enabled to purſue theſe vermin into their lurking holes and hiding places, which they generally do, and thereby at once deſtroy the whole progeny.

But the Americans, one and all, have ſuch an averſion and antipathy to the very appearance of the whole ſpecies, that notwithſtanding this kind of ſerpents are abſolutely harmleſs, and indeed extremely ſerviceable for the purpoſes juſt mentioned,

tioned, yet they are as eager to kill and deſtroy them, as the moſt noxious, virulent, and deleterious of the ſpecies, the rattle, moccaſſon, and horn-ſnakes.

I have heard many ſtrange relations of the power of ſnakes, in charming birds, and drawing them down out of the air, to devour them, by a certain faſcination in their eyes. To theſe tales I formerly gave no credit; but I have now had conviction of their truth, by frequent ocular demonſtration.

I have obſerved a little bird, fluttering in the air, within a ſmall compaſs, gradually deſcending until it came down on a buſh, then hopping from ſpray to ſpray, every time lower, conſtantly ſending forth a tremulous, doleful note, expreſſive of dread and ſurpriſe, until at length it would drop into the jaws of a ſnake on the ground, that was gaping open ready to devour it.

On ſuch occaſions, I always ſtruck the ſnake, and the inſtant he moved, the bird

bird became liberated from his fascination, flying away with the greateſt alertneſs, and would chirp, and ſoar over my head in the air, for ſome little diſtance, as if grateful for its deliverance from ſo formidable an enemy. This very extraordinary circumſtance I have taken particular notice of ſeveral different times.

Squirrels of many various kinds abound prodigiouſly, but the grey fox-ſquirrels are the moſt plenty, and moſt common: you may ſee them any where in the woods, and at any time, jumping from tree to tree, and making moſt aſtoniſhing leaps, often fifteen, twenty, and ſometimes thirty feet, from one branch to another. Theſe are the largeſt, but the flying-ſquirrel, though much ſmaller, jumps twice as far; and indeed he takes ſuch prodigious vaults, that he ſeems to fly, and appears to have wings, but they are only an expanſion of ſome looſe ſkin on each ſide of him, which affords him ſome little ſupport in the air, and breaks his fall when he miffes his hold, which indeed is very feldom.

The moft beautiful of the whole fpecies is the ground fquirrel, which is fmall, and moft delicately ftriped with contrafts of darker and lighter fhades,

CHAP. VIII.

Quality and Appearance of Soil. Wheat. Indian-Corn. Tobacco. Petersburg. Falls of Appamattox. Blandford. Pokahuntas. Indian Emperor's Daughter. Randolph and Bolling Families. The River Appamattox.

THE most commanding and excellent situations about Richmond are, the seat of a Mr. Adams, on the summit of the hill which over-looks the town; and Belvidera, an elegant villa belonging to the late colonel William Bird, of Westover, who formerly possessed a princely fortune in America, and was almost the sole proprietor of all the land adjoining the falls, for many miles, even above Westham.

Just below the falls there are very lucrative fisheries, on each side of the river; as there are many more on the James in different places, that yield great profit to the owners.

On the south side are most valuable mills and iron-works, which are worked by by means of a canal, cut from the adjoining falls of the James.

The low grounds on the James are extremely rich and fertile, producing vaſt quantities of Indian-corn, wheat, and tobacco. The ſoil is of a dark rediſh colour, and one foot and a half deep pure loam.

The high land is of an inferior quality, yet ſufficiently fertile to produce good crops of tobacco, wheat, and Indian corn; ſome of it is of a rediſh colour, mixed with clay, which is the beſt; and the worſt is of a light brown, intermixed with ſand.

The low grounds yield an increaſe in wheat of twenty-five, thirty, and ſometimes thirty-five buſhels, from one of ſeed: the high land from eight to fifteen for one. This is generally the produce of one acre. Much about the ſame quantity of Indian corn is produced from an acre, according to the quality and excellence of the ſoil, though it does not require

quire more than a peck of feed to plant it. The produce of an acre, in the culture of tobacco, in the beft land, is about fixteen hundred and fixty pounds weight: on the worft, about five hundred pounds weight. An acre always contains nearly twelve hundred and fifty hills of Indian-corn, with two, three, and fometimes, in ftrong land, four ftalks in each hill; or about five thoufand plants of tobacco.

Above the falls, the high land becomes again tolerably level, and is equal in height to the fummit of the firft hills.

The towns of Richmond and Shokoes are in Henrico county; and Chefterfield, or Rocky Bridge, is in the county of Chefterfield.

On the twenty-eighth of Auguft, I fet out on a journey to the fouthward, and as there is no fuch thing as poft-chaifes to be obtained in all America to hire, and not having furnifhed myfelf with horfes at Richmond, becaufe I was informed that I could purchafe them much better and cheaper at Peterfburg, which was about

twenty-

twenty-five miles diſtant, and directly in my way, I rode a horſe of Mr. ——'s, who preſſed me to make uſe of him.

I was fortunate in the company of a Mr. Buchanan, who was alſo going as far as Peterſburg. We croſſed the James in the ferry-boat, early in the morning, rode through the towns of Rocky-bridge, and Warwick, which is about five miles from it.

We halted at a town named Oſborn's, eight miles farther on, to bait our horſes, after paſſing Cheſterfield county court-houſe, and a church, or chapel, at this little town. Here we dined, and in the afternoon, mounting our horſes, we arrived at Blandford, having croſſed the Appamattox river, on a lofty wooden bridge, at the town of Pokahuntas.

Here we put up at Boyd's, which is the beſt houſe of public entertainment in the place.

I ſhall never forget the prodigious and inceſſant noiſe and clamour that continually aſſailed my ears, during the whole of this day's day's ride, proceeding from the green-frogs, and a multitude of other large infects on the trees, and the bull-frogs in the fwamps and places of water, on both fides of the road. I was perpetually queftioning Mr. Buchanan if they were not birds; and was aftonifhed that I could not pofsibly difcover one of them: but the noife of the bull-frogs was abfolutely tremendous.

Here, at the falls of the river Appamattox, are three towns, *viz*. Blandford, Peterfburg, and Pokahuntas.

Over the river, juft below the falls, there is a large wooden bridge, at the town of Pokahuntas which ftands on the north fide of the river named after the daughter of the famed Indian emperor, or chief, Powhattan (which is alfo the Indian appellation of the river James), who gave all the land around this place, as a portion in marriage, with his daughter Pokahuntas, to an anceftor of the prefent Randolph and Bolling families, from which ancient royal blood, a branch
of

of the Randolphs, and the whole of the Bollings (two of the moſt reſpectable houſes in Virginia), are actually deſcended.

On the ſouth ſide of the river is the town of Peterſburg, ſituated under a hill, amongſt rocks, and is extremely unhealthy.

A little diſtance, perhaps half a mile below, on the ſouth ſide alſo of the Appamattox, ſtands the charming pretty town of Blandford, in a beautiful plain, on the river brink, on a very pleaſant and delightful ſpot.

The town of Pokahuntas is in Cheſterfield county; Peterſburg is in the county of Dinwiddie, in the lower corner; and Blandford ſtands in the upper end of Prince George's county; but neither of them is a county-town.

The principal tobacco trade in America centers at Peterſburg, or Bolling's Point, which it is generally called, from the name of a family (a branch of whoſe origin I have juſt related), to which the

greater

greater part of the town and adjoining lands belong.

'It is something remarkable, that no child born at this place ever grew up to maturity, excepting the present proprietor, Mr. Bolling, whose seat over-looks Petersburg and the adjacent country and river; which is occasioned by the insalubrity of the air, and the extreme unhealthiness of the situation.

There are also some valuable mills in the vicinity of this place, erected by Mr. Bannister, a very public spirited man, who resides in an elegant house near Petersburg, which are carried on by means of a canal, cut from the neighbouring falls of the Appamattox.

The Appamattox is a small river, much about the size of the Thames, and runs into the James at City Point, about twelve miles, in a direct line, below Blandford. Sailing vessels, sloops, schooners, and flats, or lighters, come up to the bridge at the falls; but ships of burden take in their cargoes five and eight miles below.

In

In Blandford I found an excellent ordinary at Boyd's, and a tolerably agreeable mixed company of ladies and gentlemen. Amongſt the reſt, were a couple of old gentlemen, one of whom was a major in the army, with gay young wives, who did not ſeem altogether at eaſe, nor, in all probability, had they every reaſon to be ſo: however, they afforded us diverſion and entertainment enough to obſerve their various manœuvres on both ſides, or rather on all ſides; for each of the four appeared to be a commander in chief, and to have different purſuits and objects in view.

CHAP. IX.

General Character, and great Hospitality of the Virginians. Number of Inhabitants in Virginia.

THE Virginians are generous, extremely hospitable, and possess very liberal sentiments.

There is a greater distinction supported between the different classes of life here, than perhaps in any of the rest of the colonies; nor does that spirit of equality, and levelling principle, which pervades the greatest part of America, prevail to such an extent in Virginia.

However, there appears to be but three degrees of rank amongst all the inhabitants, exclusive of the negroes.

The first consists of gentlemen of the best families and fortunes in the colony, who are here much more respectable and numerous than in any other province in America. These in general have had a liberal education, possess enlightened understandings, and a thorough knowledge of the world, that furnishes them with an ease and freedom of manners and conversation, highly to their advantage in exterior, which no vicissitude of fortune or place can divest them of; they being actually, according to my ideas, the most agreeable and best companions, friends, and neighbours, that need be desired.

The greater number of them keep their carriages, and have handsome services of plate; but they all, without exception, have studs, as well as sets of elegant and beautiful horses.

Those of the second degree in rank are very numerous, being perhaps half the inhabitants, and consist of such a variety, singularity, and mixture of characters, that the exact general criterion and leading feature can scarcely be ascertained.

However, they are generous, friendly, and hospitable in the extreme; but mixed with such an appearance of rudeness, ferocity, and haughtiness, which is in fact only a want of polish, occasioned by

their

their deficiences in education, and in knowledge of mankind, as well as by their general intercourse with slaves, over whom they are accustomed to exercise an harsh and absolute command.

Many of them possess fortunes superior to some of the first rank, but their families are not so ancient, nor respectable; a circumstance here held in some estimation.

'They are all excessively attached to every species of sport, gaming, and dissipation, particularly horse-racing, and that most barbarous of all diversions, that peculiar species of cruelty, cock-fighting.

In short, take them all together, they form a strange combination of incongruous contradictory qualities, and principles directly opposite; the best and the worst, the most valuable and the most worthless, elegant accomplishments and savage brutality, being in many of them most unaccountably blended.

Yet indeed, notwithstanding this apparent inconsistency of character, principle, and conduct, numbers of them are truly valuable members of society, and few, or none, deficient in the excellencies of the intellectual faculties, and a natural genius, which, though in a great measure unimproved, is generally bright and splendid in an uncommon degree.

The third, or lower class of the people (who ever compose the bulk of mankind), are in Virginia more few in number, in proportion to the rest of the inhabitants, than perhaps in any other country in the universe. Even these are kind, hospitable, and generous; yet illiberal, noisy, and rude.

They are much addicted to inebriety, and averse to labour.

They are likewise over-burdened with an impertinent and insuperable curiosity, that renders them peculiarly disagreeable and troublesome to strangers: yet these undesirable qualities they possess by no means in an equal degree with the generality of the inhabitants of New England, whose religion and government have

United States of America.

have encouraged, and indeed inſtituted and eſtabliſhed, a kind of inquiſition, of forward impertinence and prying intruſion, againſt every perſon that may be compelled to paſs through that troubleſome, illiberal country: from which deſcription, however, there are no doubt many exceptions.

To communicate an idea of the general hoſpitality that prevails in Virginia, and indeed through all the ſouthern provinces, it may not be improper to repreſent ſome peculiar cuſtoms that are univerſal; for inſtance:

If a traveller, even a negroe, obſerves an orchard full of fine fruit, either apples or peaches, in, or near his way, he alights, without ceremony, and fills his pockets, or even a bag, if he has one, without aſking permiſſion; and if the proprietor ſhould ſee him, he is not in the leaſt offended, but makes him perfectly welcome, and aſſiſts him in chooſing out the fineſt fruit.

But this is less to be admired at, when it is considered that there is no sale here for any kind of fruit, and the finest peaches imaginable are so abundant, that the inhabitants daily feed their hogs with them during the season.

In the time of pressing cyder, if a traveller should call, to enquire his way, he is generally offered as much fine cyder as he can drink, is frequently requested to stay all night, and made heartily drunk in the bargain, if he chooses it.

When a person of more genteel figure than common calls at an ordinary (the name of their inns), for refreshment and lodging for a night, as soon as any of the gentlemen of fortune in the neighbourhood hears of it, he either comes for him himself, or sends him a polite and pressing invitation to his house, where he meets with entertainment and accommodation, infinitely superior, in every respect, to what he could have received at the inn. If he should happen to be fatigued with travelling, he is treated in

the

the moſt hoſpitable and genteel manner; and his ſervants and horſes alſo fare plenteouſly, for as long a time as he chooſes to ſtay. All this is done with the beſt grace imaginable, without even a hint being thrown out of a curioſity or wiſh to know his name.

However, it muſt be acknowledged, that many of the ſecond, and almoſt all the lower claſs of the people, are ignorant in the extreme.

Their ſentiments, and all their ideas are illiberal, narrow, and contracted; occaſioned by their inactive ſituation, confined to a ſmall compaſs, and very limited ſphere of knowledge, wherein the ſame objects are ever preſented to their view, without any variation, change, or novelty, being thereby precluded from a more general intercourſe with the world, and the different members of ſociety at large.

About the commencement of the late unfortunate diſturbances, and inauſpicious hoſtilities, the American congreſs pretended

tended to have a calculation made of the numbers of all the inhabitants in each province and colony included within their domination, which they publifhed.

But I have always concluded that oftenfible enumeration of theirs to be greatly exaggerated, purpofely to magnify their refources, numbers, and prowefs.

In that oftentatious calculation, Virginia was reprefented to contain fix hundred and fifty thoufand inhabitants; of which near two-thirds are blacks.

I computed the true number of fouls in Virginia to be then about five hundred thoufand in the whole, with a fimilar proportion of flaves included; and they have certainly decreafed in population fince that time.

CHAP.

CHAP. X.

A wretched Situation. Nottoway-River. Horses refuse to eat Bacon. Troublesome Companion. Mahirrin-River.

I Purchased two horses at Petersburg; for the best I gave fifteen pounds, the worst cost me twenty-five pounds; and a negro boy, whose price was forty pounds.

I began to prepare for my journey southward, having had the honour to visit, by invitation, several of the principal families in and near this place, among whom were Mr. Buchanan's, Mr. Bolling's, Mr. Bannister's, Mr. Eppes's, Mr. Bland's, &c.

I took my departure from Blandford, on the fourth of September, in company with a young lad from North Carolina, then on his return.

After having rode about fifteen miles we stopped to bait our horses, and dine, at

Hattan's

Hattan's ordinary, where the fare was ordinary indeed, and very indifferent.

The day being extremely hot and sultry, it was rather late in the afternoon before we set out again on our journey, and by that means I was prevented from reaching Stewart's ordinary; the house I intended to put up at that night; for being taken very ill, and as it was growing dark, I was obliged to take shelter in a shell of a house, wherein an overseer lived, and five or six negroes besides.

The young man from Carolina left me here, and continued on his journey.

My accommodation at this wretched place was miserable indeed, and it was fortunate for me, that I found myself better in the morning, or I might have been in actual danger of perishing for want of common necessaries, if my sickness had detained me therein.

If my situation, but for one night, was so intolerable, what must his be, whose constant residence it was?

It

It is indeed hardly to be conceived in what an uncomfortable ſtate that poor forlorn young man, the overſeer, then lived.

There might be about fifty acres of land cleared of woods, and chiefly under culture for Indian corn.

There was not another houſe nor hut upon the plantation, nor a ſingle fruit-tree.

' That miſerable ſhell, a poor apology for a houſe, confiſted but of one ſmall room, which ſerved for the accommodation of the overſeer and ſix negroes: it was not lathed nor plaiſtered, neither ceiled nor lofted above, and only very thin boards for its covering; it had a door in each ſide, and one window, but no glaſs in it; it had not even a brick chimney, and, as it ſtood on blocks about a foot above upon the ground, the hogs lay conſtantly under the floor, which made it ſwarm with fleas; water was near half a mile diſtant, and that very bad; there was not a neighbour within

within five miles on one side, and eight miles on the other; no book, no convenience, no furniture, no comfort in the house, unless you call by that name a miserable thin chaff bed, somewhat raised from the floor, in a corner of the room, which alternately served him for his chair, his table, and his couch.

In this wretched habitation I had little sleep, and no refreshment, although the poor young man permitted me to lie on his bed alone, and did not come there himself, but lay on the floor with the negroes; for they were shelling Indian-corn with their hands all the former part of the night, when their songs kept me awake; and the disagreeable idea of such a parcel of nasty black devils, all snoring in the same room with me, with the assistance of the musketoes, prevented me from sleep until day-break, when I arose, and having gratified the poor inhabitants of this mansion of misery with a trifle, I mounted my horse, and pursued my journey.

This morning I crossed over a pretty river named Nottoway, at Swede's-bridge, which is constructed of timber. There is some very good land on this river, both low grounds and high; it is what is called mulattoe land by the planters, from its colour.

This river is here about as large as the Thames at Kew, but is much incumbered with wood and fallen trees, brought down by the floods.

I arrived at Stewart's ordinary to breakfast, which was toasted Indian hoe-cake, and very excellent cyder, after a ride this morning of about eleven miles.

Being always particularly careful of my horses, and they having fared very indifferently the night before, I ordered the hostler to give them plenty of meat. The man stared at me, and asked me if they would eat it? Being somewhat irritated at his seeming impertinence, and out of humour by fatigue, indisposition, and want of rest, I answered, that I desired he would make the experiment, and immediately

mediately, turning away from him, went into the houſe.

In a few minutes, on looking out at the window, I was much ſurpriſed to find all the people of the place in the road before the door; and going out to enquire into the cauſe of their aſſembling there, I met the hoſtler and my boy, with each a large piece of bacon in his hand, telling me the horſes would not eat a morſel of it.

They acquainted me, that it was to ſee the horſes eat meat, by which they underſtood *bacon*, that excited the people' curioſity, and had drawn them forth into the road. I laughed heartily, and directed the hoſtler, ſince the poor ſilly horſes could not be prevailed on to taſte his bacon, to give them whatever elſe they would chooſe to eat, and as much of it as they pleaſed.

By the bye, it was a great inconvenience, and extremely troubleſome, that my boy, being an African, was of very little ſervice to me; for he ſcarcely understood a single word that I said to him, nor did I know one syllable of his language.

This ridiculous affair induced one Andrew T———, who pretended to be a humourist, to make me an offer of the honour of his company, as he was then on his way to Halifax town, in North Carolina, where he resided. His exterior being to my taste peculiarly forbidding, I declined his proposal, having no inclination to such an acquaintance. But in this I was egregiously mistaken, and altogether disappointed: Mr. T——— was not to be repulsed with such facility: he was determined to amuse himself at my expence, and at my ignorance of the customs of his country, and I was almost compelled to suffer his company, for I certainly did not accept it, but endeavoured my utmost to avoid that honour.

I told him, that as it threatened rain, I would not risque getting wet, but intended to stay some time, the length of which

which, however, might be uncertain. Well, so would Mr. T——.

When I found this, I determined to set out in the rain, which had now come on; and actually did so to avoid his company; but Mr. T—— would accommodate himself to every change of my mind, and he departed along with me.

When I rode fast, so did he; when slow, he went slow also: at length I turned short from him, along a path on the right, but my stupid servant continued to accompany Mr. T——; this obliged me to return, and gallop very fast to overtake him, as he had thereby got some miles before me.

But descending a declivity too rapidly, and without caution, the road being on clay very wet and slippery, my horse fell down with me in three-parts speed, by which I was excessively dirted, as well as hurt.

Having remounted, and rode on again, I cut a most wretched figure, being
daubed

daubed from head to foot with red clay, besides the farther injuries I had received from contusions by the fall.

In this ridiculous plight I overtook them: Mr. T—— fell a laughing fit to burst his sides, which act of rudeness and ill manners I did not seem to notice; but was much incensed at my stupid black, yet could not make him understand my expressions of resentment. This greatly encreased Mr. T——'s diversion, and ill-timed noisy mirth.

In this disagreeable condition, and uncourtly guise, we crossed a considerable stream of water, named the Three Creeks, on three wooden bridges; and a considerable river named Maherrin, larger than the Thames, at Hicks's bridge which is remarkably lofty, and built of timber, as all in the southern part of America appear to be; having passed a fine plantation, the seat of Mr. Willis, a man of fortune, and proprietor of the original stock of extraordinary swift horses, for which this part of America is noted, that vanquish all others in quarter-racing.

About thirty miles higher up, on the side of this river, near one Ingram's plantation, there have been lately discovered some very valuable medicinal springs of mineral waters, which have already performed many most remarkable and astonishing cures on persons afflicted with various kinds of lameness, infirmity, and disease, who annually resort to these springs, from an hundred and fifty miles around.

We took some refreshment at Edwards's ordinary, an exceeding good building, with excellent accommodations, lately erected at this place, which is exactly twenty-eight miles north from Halifax, in North Carolina, and forty-seven south from Petersburg in Virginia.

We rested but a very short time here, and, although it continued to rain fast, proceeded on our journey.

At the distance of ten miles from Hicks's bridge and ford, we entered the province of North Carolina, and three miles

miles farther on, croffed a large ftream of water named Fountain's creek, fifteen miles north of Halifax town, which we reached that night, after croffing the river Roanoak, in a flat ferry boat, on the fouth bank of which the town is built.

Towards the conclufion of this day's ride, I had the fatisfaction of retorting the laugh on Mr. T—— very handfomely, for his horfe tumbled down, and fairly rolled him in the mire, all over, three times moft completely.

He was in fuch a ridiculous condition and lamentable plight, being befides a moft unwieldy, uncouth figure, that you could fcarcely difcover whether the creature was human or not; nor would it have been poffible for the moft rigid Cynic to refrain from immoderate laughter, at beholding his rueful countenance, and wretched guife.

This was a moft unpleafant journey; bad accommodation, bad roads, bad company and attendance, and, in fhort, every thing difagreeable in the extreme.

G 2 CHAP.

CHAP. XI.

North Carolina. Halifax Town. Roanoak-River. Falls. Rock Fight. Floods.

HALIFAX is a pretty town on the south side of the Roanoak (a river larger, or at least containing more water than the James), about eight miles below the first falls, and near fifty miles higher up than the tide flows; but sloops, schooners, and flats, or lighters, of great burden, come up to this town against the stream, which is deep and gentle.

Halifax enjoys a tolerable share of commerce in tobacco, pork, butter, flour, and some tar, turpentine, skins, furs, and cotton.

There are many handsome buildings in Halifax and its vicinity, but they are almost all constructed of timber, and painted white; among them are Mr. Mountfort's, Mr. Abner Nash's, Mr. Martin's (now an ordinary, or inn, built by, and formerly the refidence of a Mr. Elmſley, an eminent practitioner in the law), Mr. Long's, Mr. Eaton's, and Mr. Jones's; the laſt is in Occoneachy-neck, an extreme rich and valuable tract of land, about two miles from town, and is indeed an elegant feat.

Halifax is twenty-five miles due fouth from Peterſburg, and one hundred from Richmond, is the capital of a diſtrict, and the county-town of Halifax county.

In and around the town the foil is fandy; the banks of the river on the fouth fide are high, but low on the north, and very fubject to inundations, fo remarkably, that the ferry-houfe, a wooden building, which ſtands on that fide, is obliged to be faſtened with ropes, tied to the trees, to prevent it from being waſhed away by the floods.

The quantity of water that comes down the Roanoak, on fuch occafions, is indeed amazing and enormous; trees, fences, corn, tobacco, horfes, cattle, and even houfes, houses, are all swept away by the torrent, and caried down with the stream.

There is a singular phenomenon attends this river, which is, that during days, or seasons of rain, it does not rise any thing, or but very little beyond the common magnitude; but two or three days after the rain has ceased, when the sky and sun are again become bright and fine, and the bad weather is forgotten, then, and not before, the Roanoak begins to swell, and encreases with such rapidity and violence, that the inhabitants have scarcely time to drive their cattle, horses, sheep, hogs, &c. off from the low-grounds up to the high, before the whole are overflowed; and without this precaution all their live stock would be swept away and destroyed, which frequently happens, notwithstanding every exertion and care.

There is another peculiarity attends this river; that is, the low grounds are generally higher, next the river side, than where they adjoin the high-land; thus,

by

by means of guts, communicating from the river to the back part of the low-grounds, which is moſt commonly a miry ſwamp with cauſeways over it, the water of the floods is ſoon brought there, by which the retreat of every living creature is cut off in a very ſhort time after the waters begin to encreaſe, and conſequently all included within muſt inevitably periſh, ſhould the inundation overſpread the whole.

However, the floods ſeldom cover every ſpot, there being ſome particular places in the low grounds conſiderably higher than the reſt, which, on ſuch occaſions, are crowded with the poor terrified animals: but once every two or three years the Roanoak ſwells ſeveral feet above the higheſt of thoſe places.

The Roanoak, or as it is ſometimes called, the Morattuck, is above a quarter of a mile over at Halifax, but very deep, and is much wider many miles above. It empties itſelf into Albemarle Sound, at Edinton, where it is ſeven miles wide, and receives on the north fide, the Chowan-River, or Sound; which is formed by the confluence of the three rivers, Maherrin, Nottoway, and Blackwater, and is something more than two miles in breadth.

The communication with the sea, from this enormous body of water, is through Roanoak inlet, where there is a bar, fluctuating banks, and shifting quick-sands, that prevent ships of burden from entering this extensive bay.

I put up at Martin's, the best house of public entertainment in Halifax.

Here I disposed of my black boy, who was in fact totally useless to me; but I gained ten pounds by my bargain.

From this place I made many excursions around it, and had the honour of visiting, by invitation, every family of note, for a considerable distance in the vicinity.

Being one of a party that was to pass some days on a jaunt in the country, I proposed calling to take a view of the
falls

falls of Roanoak. We were accompanied by Charles Eaton, efq. and Mr. W. Park, whofe feats are in the neighbourhood of thefe falls.

There was nothing remarkable to be obferved in them, only a prodigious body of water, dafhing and tumbling over rocks: but to thofe who have feen the falls of the James, thefe are no object.

There is a very extraordinary circumftance, however, attends thefe falls every fpring, about the eighth of May; it is called the rock fight. This is occafioned by fuch amazing numbers of thofe fifhes, here called Bafs-Rocks, coming up to the falls at the fame time to fpawn, that a dog thrown into the river then, would not be able to fwim acrofs, nor could live in it one quarter of an hour: you may actually fee them crowded thick upon each other, even to the furface of the water.

This fingular phenomenon continues for three days, but on one of thefe days, in particular,

particular, the agitation of the water is most violent, the whole river being in a foam.

There are many valuable fisheries at, and in the vicinity of Halifax, below the falls, on each side of the river.

During this excursion we called at Mount Pleasant, the seat of ——— Dawson, esq. on the banks of the Roanoak, about eighteen miles above Halifax, and in returning stayed some days at the seats of Mr. Eaton, and Mr. Park.

About a mile out of Halifax town is a creek named Quankey (the Indian appellation for red paint, with which it abounds), with an exceeding lofty bridge thrown over it, built of timber, on the south side of which is the seat of a Mr. Nicholas Long, where we frequently walked out in the mornings and evenings to drink cow's milk, which was there excellent.

About five or six miles farther on, in the same direction, is a considerable settlement, upon a pretty large water-course, named the

the Marsh, where we several times went, on invitation from Alexander M'Colloch, esq. a gentleman of considerable note, and Archibald Hamilton, esq.* a merchant of eminence, who carried on a very extensive and valuable commerce in Virginia, as well as in North Carolina; and we were entertained with great hospitality and politeness by each of them.

We visited Willie Jones, esq. doctor Cathcart's, William Williams, esq. &c. among many other gentlemen's seats, and met with a most courteous and friendly reception from all.

* This gentleman's brother, lieutenant colonel John Hamilton, is now in the British service, and commanded a provincial corps, named the North Carolina loyalists, having behaved with great gallantry, both under the earl of Cornwallis and lord Rawdon.

CHAP.

CHAP. XII.

Lofty Timber. Method of clearing Land. Woods on Fire. Dreadful Conflagrations.

THE low grounds of Roanoak are extremely rich and fertile, but in general too light and sandy for the culture of wheat, which here grows much too luxuriant and high, whereby it falls and lodges before the ears fill and ripen.

The soil is a fine black loam, for several feet deep, and is indeed inexhaustible, but extremely subject to inundations, which sweep away whole inclosures, as well as the crops, and often leave the land covered with wrecks of the flood, and incumbered with vast quantities of large trees, brought down by the torrent.

The low-grounds are generally from a quarter to a mile wide; and it is observable, for the whole length of the Roanoak, that the low-grounds are always

ways on one side of the river only, never on both together, but still promiscuously: thus, when the low grounds are on the north side, there are high lands on the south; and where the low grounds are on the south side, the land on the north side is high, almost flush to the brink of the river. It is remarkable also, that wherever the high lands join the river, they are rich and fertile, but where they join the low grounds only, they are of a very inferior quality.

The timber is of an immense bulk on the low grounds, and consists of white and yellow poplars, black wallnut, hornbeam, red bud, sweet gum, dog wood, sycamores, oaks, ash, beech, elm, &c. On the rich high land, it consists of hickory, sassafrass, oaks, &c. and on the inferior high land, of lofty pines, of a great height, mixed with scrubby oaks, black-gum, and maple.

In this part of America there are seven different species of oak, viz. black-oak,

white-

white-oak, red-oak, Spanish-oak, willow-oak, live-oak, and scrubby oak.

The appearance and colour of the soil in the best high lands, is dark brown, with a slight tinge of red, and covered with tall timber. That of the worst is whitish-brown, either very sandy and light, or stiff, wet, and livery, with low, crooked timber, excepting the pines, which generally grow large, tall, and straight every where, unless they are crowded together. But the worst timber, on the worst land, makes a better appearance, and is larger than the trees in St. James's and Hyde-parks.

The general mode of clearing the land in this country, where timber is of no value, and labour is of great, is by cutting a circle round the tree, through the bark, quite to the wood, before the sap rises, which kills it; and they cultivate the ground below immediately, leaving the trees to rot standing, which happens within a very few years, and they never bear leaves more.

A large

A large field in this situation, makes a moſt ſingular, ſtriking, and tremendous appearance: it would ſeem indeed dangerous to walk in it, as the trees are of a prodigious height and magnitude; vaſt limbs, and branches of enormous ſize impending in awful ruins, from a great height, ſometimes breaking off, and frequently whole trees falling to the ground, with a horrible craſh, the ſound of which is increaſed and protracted by the reverberation of the ſurrounding echoes. Yet, notwithſtanding this apparent danger, very few accidents ever happen from it. I never heard of any excepting to beaſts.

When the timber is cut down, or falls, they ſaw the ſmaller trees in pieces, and heap them up together in huge piles, and in many different places, where they ſet fire to them in the winter, at which time the whole country around appears in a blaze; and the atmoſphere is then extremely incommoded, and totally pervaded with ſmoak.

For

For very frequently the large, dry, and almost rotten standing timber, catches fire, and blazes with great fury: the fire is also communicated to the leaves on the ground, in the surrounding woods, which are there accumulated to a great depth, by falling from the trees to the earth, where they have been encreasing, *stratum super stratum*, from the most remote period of time; being very dry and combustible, they instantly catch fire like tinder; the conflagration quickly spreads many miles on every side, and at length becomes general and dreadfully tremendous; for there is no possibility of extinguishing, or restraining the violence and velocity of the devouring flames, which destroy and consume fences, inclosures, timber, and all vegetation; driving even the wild beasts before them in flocks; and their progress, at length, is only terminated by some large river, or by heavy rains.

This

This has induced the legiflature to endeavour to guard againft fuch alarming accidents, by paffing acts to prevent fetting fire to the woods, &c. notwithftanding which, thefe terrible conflagrations are ftill frequent every year.

CHAP. XIII.

Inhabitants of the Country and of the Towns. Classes of People. Stores. Planters. Methods of Trade and Commerce.

THE inhabitants of this part of America may be comprehended in a very few classes.

All in the country, without exception, are planters, store-keepers or persons in trade, and hunters: these last are chiefly confined to the back country and frontiers next the Indians.

In the towns there are some few mechanics, surgeons, lawyers, store-keepers or persons in the commercial line, and tavern-keepers.

However, the generality of the towns are so inconsiderable, that in England they would scarcely acquire the appellation of villages.

The different distinct branches of manufacturers, such as hosiers, haberdashers, clothiers,

clothiers, linen-drapers, grocers, stationers, &c. are not known here; they are all comprehended in the single name and occupation of merchant, or storekeeper.

What are called shops in England, are known here by the appellation of stores, and supply the inhabitants with every individual article necessary in life, such as linens, woollens, silks, paper, books, iron, cutlery, hats, stockings, shoes, wines, spirits, sugars, &c. and even jewelry; for which in return they receive tobacco, skins, furs, cotton, butter, flour, &c. in considerable quantities at a time, being obliged to give a year's credit.

By this it appears, that there is but little specie in circulation; indeed there is no great occasion for it; for a planter raises his own meats, beef, and bacon, his own corn and bread, his drink, cyder, and brandy, his fruit, apples, peaches, &c. and great part of his cloathing, which is cotton.

He has no market to repair to but the neareſt ſtore; which chiefly ſupplies him with finery, beſides the uſeful and neceſſary articles for agriculture, and what little clothing his ſlaves require, for which he pays his crop of tobacco, or whatever elſe may be his ſtaple produce, and is always twelve months in arrear.

CHAP.

CHAP. XIV.

Tarburg. Attacked by an itinerant New-light Preacher. Got Lost. Strange Ignorance and uncouth Appearance of the Inhabitants. Instance of extraordinary Hospitality and Benevolence. Chowan Sound. Moccosson Snakes. Rattle-Snakes. Cure for their Bite.

I Made an excursion to a little town, named Tarburg: it is not half so large as Halifax, being a very insignificant place indeed.

I was entertained by a Mr. Hall, the night I remained in this place, and returned to Halifax next day.

Tarburg is about forty miles due south from Halifax, and has not been built many years.

The chief produce around this place is tar, Indian corn, and hogs.

There is a large wooden bridge over Tar-river, at this town, which is very high and wide, yet several as good have been carried away by the floods.

I made another peregrination, which on account of the singularity of the adventures therein, I shall relate.

It was to Chowan-sound.

I set out from Halifax, and rode along down the south side of the Roanoak, as far as Pulham's ferry (about fifteen miles below the town), where I crossed the river, and that evening reached Matthew Brickle's ordinary.

Here I found tolerable accommodations, but had to defend myself against the formidable attacks of a new-light itinerant preacher, who had perverted this family, as well as most of the inhabitants in the vicinity; and after exhausting all the fire of his artillery, cant, and pretended inspiration, upon me in vain, he very gravely and formally concluded, and pronounced with great solemnity, that I was an obstinate unbeliever, and that my hour of receiving light and divine grace was not yet arrived.

Having rode thirty-six miles that day, I set out next morning, and proceeded
through

through the dreary pines, which compose almost all the woods that grow down this way; and about twelve o'clock, following a path that led me out of my road, I got entirely bewildered and lost.

Being extremely fatigued, hungry, and dry, I called at several miserable hovels, at the distances of five or six miles asunder, but could neither obtain directions on my way, or any kind of refreshment; even the water was so very ill tasted, and insalubrious, that it could scarcely be drank.

I rode on in this miserable dilemma and precarious situation, among these ignorant wretches, until night approached, when they all refused to permit me to lodge under their shelters: " Wonder-
" ing (as they said) where I came from,
" or why I should come there, where
" nobody comes; but (telling me) if I
" could get to Mr. Tyers's, about seven
" miles off, I might get quarters; for
" he often had strange, outlandish folks
" to lodge at his house; and was a rich
" man,

"man, and had a mill, and a black-
"smith's shop, and a still."

These people are the most wretchedly ignorant of any I ever met with. They could not tell me the name of the place, county, or parish they resided in, nor any other place in the adjacent country; neither could they furnish me with any directions, by which I might again discover and ascertain the right way.

Their appearance also is equally sordid and mean, being of a sallow complexion and yellowish hue, almost as tawney as mulattoes, with the smoak of the lightwood (the roots and knots of pine, so named here), which is their whole fuel, clothed in cotton rags, that had been once dyed of some colour, and all enveloped in dirt and nastiness.

With much persuasion, I procured one of these lumps of mortality to accompany me as a guide to this Mr. Tyers's, where, after much difficulty, and no small hazard in passing over several deep and
miry

miry swamps, I at length arrived, a little after dark.

Here I obtained ample compensation for the churlishness of those ignorant creatures whom I had been among, by the hearty welcome, and kind hospitable entertainment I received from Mr. Tyers, who appears to be a little monarch in this domain, being the only magistrate in this place for thirty miles around, and, I had almost pronounced, the only intelligent being.

His house was the seat of plenty and plainness, mirth and good-humour, and genuine hospitality without ostentation; but entirely out of the way from all public roads.

Here I found a large table loaded with fat roasted turkies, geese, and ducks, boiled fowls, large hams, hung-beef, barbicued pig, &c. enough for five-and-twenty men.

Mr. Tyers told me, that it was but seldom he was favoured with the company of any strangers; but when he was so fortunate, it always afforded him great pleasure to entertain them, because he was sensible that they could obtain no refreshment any where near him, and for that reason, he had given directions to the inhabitants for twenty miles around him, to send all strangers to his house.

Mr. Tyers, with a benevolence and grace that would do honour to any station, mounted his horse, next morning, to accompany me for the day; both to shew me the way, and the country.

We arrived at a ferry on Chowan-river, or sound (named Cotton's): it is three miles over; we crossed it, and rode along upon a wooden causeway, through a marsh, which is here called a poccoson, growing thick with tall reeds, near three miles over.

Down this way I also observed great numbers of cypress trees, tall, straight, and lofty, in many of the swamps and low grounds; besides multitudes of singular

gular excrescences, named cypress knees, which make a very odd appearance, arising in the form of knees, out of the most miry places.

We then returned, and reached my old sanctified landlord Matthew Brickle's, that night, where Mr. Tyers stayed also; and in the morning we parted: he returning to his house, the mansion of benevolence and virtue; and I to Halifax, heartily tired, and sick of my excursion.

I cannot omit observing a singular and very disagreeable sight I noticed in passing Chowan-river: it was numbers of large serpents, lying upon logs and fallen trees in the river, basking themselves in the sun.

It seems this marsh, morass, or poccoson, as such places are named here, abounds with these noxious disgustful creatures.

Most of them were of the kind called moccosson snakes, as large as the rattle-snake, but thicker, shorter, and destitute of rattles, which renders them

more

more dangerous, as by this means they bite without previous warning, which the rattle-snake never does, and their bite is equally poisonous and fatal; some say more so.

They are beautifully speckled, just in the same manner as the rattle-snake, though they appear duller, the colours of each being the same, but those of the moccossons not so bright; for the similitude between them is so very strong, that these are generally reckoned the female rattle snakes, by the more ignorant inhabitants.

Although the bite of both these snakes have always proved certain death, yet it is surprising to observe, that the inhabitants are under very slender apprehensions from them: indeed they seem to dread them no more than any other serpent.

However, all the Americans appear to have a particular antipathy to the whole species.

It has but very lately been discovered, that there is a remedy of efficacy for the
bite

bite of thofe fnakes, and an antidote againſt their poiſon.

This is equal quantities of the juice of hore-hound and plantain, adminiſtered internally, largely and frequently, and poultices of the bruiſed plants applied to the wound.

It was a poor negroe ſlave that firſt diſcovered this valuable ſovereign remedy; and the aſſembly, or parliament of North-Carolina, rewarded him with his freedom, and two hundred pounds for divulging it. A laudable example to governments, and an inſtance of their ſuperior humanity; which will for ever reflect upon them the higheſt honour.

Notwithſtanding this plain and ſimple remedy may be readily obtained, and eaſily adminiſtered by the moſt ignorant, as both horehound and plantain grow ſpontaneouſly near almoſt every houſe, and in moſt places where the land has been cleared of woods; yet the knowledge of this great benefit to be derived from them has extended but very little, oecaſioned by by the fmall intercourfe, and very limited communication there is in general between the thinly and diftantly fcattered inhabitants of this wide-fpread country: fo that from this ignorance, the bite of thefe noxious and deadly ferpents continue ftill to prove almoft as fatal as ever.

CHAP.

CHAP. XV.

Extraordinary Woman. American General an Innkeeper. Dreadful Thunder-clap. Simplicity of the Negroes. An extraordinary Instance thereof.

ABOUT the beginning of November I departed from Halifax, where with great satisfaction I had enjoyed a very agreeable society, on my route to Hillsborough, which is just one hundred and twenty-two miles distant.

I called at Edmundson's ordinary to bait my horse, and to breakfast; which is about ten or eleven miles from Halifax.

At this house I saw the largest and strongest woman, perhaps, in the world: she was six feet two inches and a half in height, well built in proportion, strong, robust, and muscular as a man of the same stature. She possessed a boldness and spirit inferior to no man; and there was no bully, bruiser, wrestler, or any person that excelled in athletic power and agility,

agility, for fifty miles around, that she had not complimented with a fair and complete drubbing; in short, she was a perfect virago, of great courage and astonishing strength and ill nature.

I submitted to some small imposition in her charge, rather than enter the lists with her in dispute, and run the risque of experiencing her prowess; for indeed this is only a contribution she constantly levies or exacts upon all that frequent this house, of which she is master as well as mistress, her insignificant husband being an absolute cypher.

Having received an invitation to spend some days with Thomas Eaton, esq. at his seat on the banks of the Roanoak, twenty-eight miles above Halifax, I arrived there to dinner.

It is pleasantly situated on the south side of the river, which is one half wider here than at Halifax.

There is a very public ferry at this place, belonging to Mr. Eaton, and of great emolument to him.

The low grounds are more extenfive here than any where elfe on the Roanoak.

Mr. Eaton poffeffes a very fine eftate: this plantation alone is worth at leaft three thoufand pounds, containing about fifteen hundred acres; yet his father purchafed the whole for thirty pounds. With fuch aftonifhing rapidity has the value of landed property increafed in this province.

During the few days that I remained at Mr. Eaton's, we made many pleafant excurfions in the vicinity, on vifits to every perfon of any note.

In a little emigration to Ofborn Jefferies's, efq. on the banks of Tar-River, my horfe falling lame, obliged us to call and make fome ftay at an ordinary, inn, or tavern, at Bute county courthoufe, kept by one Jethroe Sumner, where we found an excellent dinner as well as an agreeable facetious hoft.

[This inn-keeper has diftinguifhed himfelf in the courfe of the late war, being

Vol. I.   I   the

the general Sumner, of the American army, who has been so active in the Carolinas.

He is a man of a person lusty, and rather handsome, with an easy and genteel address: his marriage with a young woman of a good family, with whom he received a handsome fortune; his being a captain of provincials last war; but above all his violent principles, and keeping an inn at the courthouse (which is scarcely thought a mean occupation here), singular as the latter circumstance may appear, contributed more to his appointment and promotion in the American army, than any other merit.

For it is a fact, that more than one third of their general officers have been inn-keepers, and have been chiefly indebted to that circumstance for such rank.

Because by that public, but inferior station, their principles and persons became more generally known; and by the

the mixture and variety of company they converfed with, in the way of their bufinefs, their ideas and their ambitious views were more excited and extended than the generality of the honeft and refpectable planters, who remained in peace at their homes.]

There is an extreme valuable body of rich high land that extends five miles around Bute county court-houfe: this whole tract is ftrong and fertile in an uncommon degree. There is fcarcely a pine-tree to be found within that diftance, although the furrounding woods on every fide, are very much mixed with them.

Having been favoured with a kind and preffing invitation to vifit Robert Alexander, efq. I left Mr. Eaton's, and called upon him, from whom I alfo received every attention and civility.

Mr. Alexander accompanied me to view a remarkable place in the Roanoak, named the Horfe-ford; the only one where horfes can crofs the river, in that manner, for a vaſt diſtance: it is fifteen miles above Eaton's ferry, and at this place the river is more than half a mile wide: it is fordable only during one month in the drieſt ſeaſon of the year, and even then it is extremely hazardous and difficult; the water being never leſs than four feet deep, and the current very rapid.

The land on each ſide of the river at this place is broken and hilly, beſides being very ſterile and poor in quality.

The weather here, at this ſeaſon of the year, is really charming, neither too cold, nor much incommoded with heat; the air and ſky being always clear, bright, and ſerene, and thunder and ſtorms much leſs frequent.

I forgot to mention, that while I was at Mr. Eaton's, one morning having aroſe very early, ſtanding at the door, I obſerved a ſingle ſmall black cloud, and not another, of any kind, to be ſeen in the hemiſphere, the ſky being a pure bright azure: that inſtant, all on a ſudden, there

there came the moſt violent and tremendous thunder-clap that ever I remember to have heard; the lightning ſtruck Mr. Eaton's kitchen, ſplit down the chimney, performed a multitude of fantaſtic freaks of electricity, and killed two negroe men, but did no hurt to two infants, then in their arms.

This was accounted the more extraordinary, as there was only that ſingle exploſion: and in the moſt violent thunder ſtorms, when peals ſucceed each other, in loud contention, for a conſiderable duration of time, any accident happening therefrom is ſeldom ever heard of; only large, lofty trees in the woods are frequently ſplit in ſhivers, from top to bottom, and ſet on fire by the lightning on ſuch occaſions.

Both Mr. Alexander and Mr. Eaton poſſeſs excellent plantations, rich, fertile, and very valuable: they are both great and eminent planters, and value themſelves highly upon their ſkill, their induſtry, and their ſuperior crops.

At Mr. Eaton's I saw the largeſt turnip that I can recollect ever to have heard of: it was four feet eight inches in circumference, but was of the flat ſpungy kind, and not at all thick in proportion. This turnip was not cultivated alone, but grew in a large field unmanured, promiſcuouſly with many thouſands more, numbers of which were perhaps as large as this, for I meaſured it myſelf in the field.

I ſhall here relate a trifling, or rather diverting circumſtance that may be intereſting to ſome, by evincing the great ſimplicity of the blacks.

Having taken with me a negroe named Richmond, from a plantation here, which I had juſt purchaſed and ſettled, to carry me over the Roanoak in a canoe, that I might contemplate on and enjoy an elegant, wild perſpective, from the ſummit of a conſiderable eminence that aroſe abruptly on a peninſula, almoſt ſurrounded by the river, I ordered him to meet me with the canoe at the oppoſite ſide of the peninſula.

When

When I arrived there, at the time appointed, there was no canoe, and no negroe: I called out for Richmond, as loud as I could vociferate, but had no anfwer.

It was about the middle of the day, which happened to be uncommonly hot and fultry; I was much indifpofed and reduced very weak with an intermittent fever;

After waiting until the heat of the weather and the fever had almoft overcome me, I refolved to walk down, along the fide of the river, until I fhould meet or find him; as I apprehended he might be afleep, which all negroes are extremely addicted to: but in this attempt I found the utmoft difficulty, from the almoft infuperable impediments of trees fallen, and impending over the water, deep miry foil and leaves that funk to my knees every ftep, impenetrable briars and underwood, black muddy gutts from the river, which compelled me to make circuits of half a mile to get round each of them, and innumerable fwarms of musketoes, ticks, poisonous insects, and snakes.

Every quarter of a mile I loudly called him, but received no answer. Frequently quite overpowered with weakness and fatigue, I sunk down to rest, and as often, for mere self-preservation and defence, was compelled to arise again to insupportable toil. At length night overtook me, with my cloaths torn, my flesh lacerated and bleeding with briars and thorns, stung all over by poisonous insects, suffocated with thirst and heat, and fainting under fatigue, imbecility, and disease.

In this wretched miserable condition, I at length arrived at the place where I had landed in the morning, having travelled about five miles in seven hours, through a perpetual thicket of almost impenetrable woods.

Here I found Richmond, fast asleep in the canoe, exactly in the same spot where I had left him in the morning.

Being incensed in the highest degree, I threatened him with severe punishment,
when

when he begged me to liften to his excufe.
' Kay maffa (fays he), you juft leave
' me, me fit here, great fifh jump up
' into de canoe; here he be, maffa, fine
' fifh, maffa; me den very grad; den
' me fit very ftill, until another great fifh
' jump into de canoe; but me fall afleep,
' maffa, and no wake till you come:
' now, maffa, me know me deferve flog-
' ging, caufe if great fifh did jump into
' de canoe, he fee me afleep, den he
' jump out again, and I no catch him;
' fo, maffa, me willing now take good
' flogging.'——

My pain and vexation were for a moment forgotten, and I laughed heartily at the poor fellow's ignorance, and extreme fimplicity, in waiting there for more fifhes to jump into his canoe, becaufe one had happened to do fo; and therefore forgave his crime.

CHAP.

CHAP. XVI.

Nutbush Creek. Member of Congress. Anecdotes of the famous Henderson, and the Origin of the new Settlement of Kentucky.

WHEN I left Mr. Alexander's, I proceeded up the river side to Taylor's ferry, which is the most frequented of any on Roanoak, and is situated on the great road leading from the most populous parts of the Carolinas, to the richest and most thick settled division of Virginia.

I then struck out on my left hand, into a very fine settlement called Nutbush, from a creek of that name, which runs through it; and it is a large body of excellent land.

I put up at the house of a Mr. Penn, a man of some property, to whom I had been furnished with letters of recommendation and civility.

From this gentleman I received the politest attentions, and we entered on a very serious and private converfation on political fubjects, wherein he fully opened his mind, and difclofed his fentiments on that head with the moft undifguifed confidence, freedom, and candour.

[The above Mr. Penn was afterwards a delegate to Congrefs from the ftate of North Carolina; and a few days fubfequent to their declaration of independence, while I was a prifoner among the Americans, having an opportunity of converfing with him, and finding his political principles fo totally different from what they appeared to me to be before, I gave him a hint thereof, which calling back his recollection to our former confidential converfation, perfectly filenced him, fo that he actually was incapable of making any farther reply.]

Here I alfo called at one Williams's, a lawyer, who is faid to be, and is very much like a mulattoe.

At

At this house I happened to fall in company, and have a great deal of conversation with one of the most singular and extraordinary persons and excentric geniuses in America, and perhaps in the world.

His name is Nathaniel Henderson; his father is still alive, a poor man, whose residence is in the settlement of Nutbush, where he was at this time on a visit.

This son was grown up to maturity before he had been taught to read or write, and he acquired those rudiments of education, and arithmetic also, by his own indefatigable industry.

He then obtained the inferior office of constable; from that was promoted to the office of under-sheriff; after this he procured a licence to plead as a lawyer, in the inferior or county courts, and soon after in the superior, or highest courts of judicature.

Even there, where oratory and eloquence is as brilliant and powerful as in Westminster-hall, he soon became distinguished and

and eminent, and his superior genius shone forth with great splendor, and universal applause.

He was, at the same time, a man of pleasure, gay, facetious, and pliant; nor did his amazing talents, and general praise, create him a single enemy.

In short, while yet a very young man, he was promoted from the bar to the bench, and appointed Associate Chief Judge of the province of North Carolina, with a salary adequate to the dignity.

Even in this elevated station, his reputation and renown continued to increase.

But having made several large purchases, and having fallen into a train of expence that his circumstances and finances could not support, his extensive genius struck out on a bolder tract to fortune and fame, than any one had ever attempted before him.

Under pretence of viewing some back lands, he privately went out to the Cherokee nation of Indians, and, for an insignificant consideration (only ten waggons loaded with cheap goods, such as coarse woollens, trinkets, some fire-arms, and spirituous liquors), made a purchase from the chiefs of the nation, of a vast tract of territory, equal in extent to a kingdom; and in the excellence of climate and soil, extent of its rivers, and beautiful elegance of situations, inferior to none in the universe. A domain of no less than one hundred miles square, situated on the back or interior part of Virginia, and of North and South Carolina; comprehending the rivers Kentucky, Cherokee, and Ohio, besides a variety of inferior rivulets, delightful and charming as imagination can conceive.

This transaction he kept a profound secret, until such time as he obtained the final ratification of the whole nation in form. Then he immediately invited settlers from all the provinces, offering them land on the most advantageous terms, and proposing to them likewise, to form a legislature and government of their own; such as might be most convenient to their particular circumstances of settlement. And he inſtantly vacated his ſeat on the bench.

Mr. Henderſon by this means eſtabliſhed a new colony, numerous and reſpectable, of which he himſelf was actually proprietor as well as governor, and indeed legiſlator alſo; having framed a code of laws, particularly adapted to their ſingular ſituation, and local circumſtances.

In vain did the different governors fulminate their proclamations of outlawry againſt him and his people: in vain did they offer rewards for apprehending him, and forbid every perſon from joining, or repairing to his ſettlement; under the ſanction and authority of a general law, that renders the formal aſſent of the governors and aſſemblies of the different provinces abſolutely neceſſary to validate the purchaſe of any lands from the Indian nations. For this inſtance, being the act of the Indians themſelves,
they

they defended him and his colony, being in fact as a bulwark and barrier between Virginia, as well as North and South Carolina and him; his territory lying to the weftward of their nation.

I beg leave to obferve, that I do not prefume to undertake his juftification, but only admire his enterprifing policy, and the vigour and activity of his mind.

CHAP.

CHAP. XVI.

Harrisburg. Tar River. Taken Sick. Extremely ill. Uncivilized Inhabitants. Handsome Women. Instances of worse than savage Brutality. A very singular and diverting Trick. Meet with a beautiful Girl. Another singular Trick.

FROM the conversation I had with this very extraordinary person, Mr. Henderson, I entertained a strong inclination to pay a visit to his domain; which must certainly afford a large field for speculation and enterprise, being situated in the very heart of the continent of America, and in a great degree precluded from the general intercourse of the rest of mankind, and society at large, being likewise several hundred miles distant from any other settlement.

However, some misunderstandings and disturbances that I was informed had broke out between the Virginians and the Shawnese and other Indians, I apprehended would at this particular period render the enterprize rather hazardous; Mr. Henderson himself appearing rather intimidated at the danger.

Having proceeded on my journey, I slept at a place where they have dignified a few log hovels with the appellation of a town called Harrisburg, from the proprietor's name.

On the day following I forded two streams of water named Fishing Creek and Tar River, some miles distant from each other; the last of which is pretty considerable, and very rocky.

Finding myself rather indisposed, I stopped at a house on the banks of a watercourse named Napareed's Creek, and was compelled to remain there all night.

In the morning I became much worse, and soon found myself seized with a most severe sickness, here called a *Seasoning* (to the country and climate.) It was a violent bilious fever, and soon reduced me to the verge of death.

There was nothing to be procured in this place fit for a sick person, not even a nurse. Nature and a good constitution were my only physicians and medicines.

I lay

I lay for ten days quite delirious and helpless, and it was five weeks before I was out of danger; but even then, so extremely weak and low, that I was scarcely able to walk across the room.

My strength returned so very slowly, that I was obliged to make a long residence in this solitary place, but thereby I became much more familiarized with, and reconciled to the customs, conversation, and manners of the people, which, it must be confessed, are sufficiently rude and disgusting.

I also formed particular, and agreeable enough acquaintances with the softer sex; who are, to be sure, very singular in their manners and behaviour, although almost the only humanized beings in the place.

In their shape and features some of them are certainly very handsome, yet, at best, little better than beautiful savages.

But was I to relate the various instances I have seen of the extreme rudeness and brutality of many of the men, they would scarcely appear credible to the civilized part of the species.

However, I shall hazard a very few of the most moderate, by which some judgement of the rest may be formed.

They seem to entertain little or no sense of religion, and as little knowledge, or fear, of a future state, God, or Devil.

But they all, especially the women, profess an avowed partiality for Britons, whom, notwithstanding, they call outlandish folks, ignorant and unpolished, thinking themselves the only polite, knowing people in the world.

The following are some of the instances I promised to mention of their ferocity.

They cut off the ears and tail of a favourate cat of mine, and called it fun.

She had young ones, and the barbarians cut off the ears and tails of all the kittens; this they called high; and were excessively delighted at beholding the poor animals agonies and contortions in death.

I accustomed myself to go out along with them a hunting, fishing, swimming,

ming, fowling, &c. for my amusement and diversion.

Being once on a visit at a Mr. Glen's, he and I went to the river to swim, it being but a very short distance from his house; whilst we were there, his wife and her sister, who were both young and handsome, came down to the water-side, and in a frolic hid our cloaths.

After they had laughed at us for some time, they informed us where they were, and I put mine on; but he ran out of the water, and pursued the women stark naked.

Having caught his wife, he brought her into the room where her sister and I were, locked the door, took out the key, threw her down on the bed, and notwithstanding her utmost endeavours to prevent him and disengage herself, committed an act that a mere savage would have been ashamed to have attempted in public.

This he would afterwards boast of in all companies, in the presence of his wife and every other lady, as an excellent joke, and prodigious piece of humour.

I had an aversion to the fellow ever after this, and I believe his wife liked him no better; for she frequently complained to me how extremely odious he was become to her.

Soon after this I played this biped a trick, that afforded me a sufficient share of diversion at his expence.

Being in a store where Glen had just purchased a very handsome fowling-piece, I secretly took an opportunity of loading her with powder, and wadding her with spunk, charge over charge, several times, until the barrel was almost full, (spunk is a fungous substance that grows on the oak, which catches fire like tinder, and consumes slowly, until it communicates the fire to whatever it touches.)

After he had mounted his horse to go home, I dropped a spark of fire into the muzzle of his gun as I handed her up to him.

He then rode on very quietly, followed at a little distance by me and another person, to whom I had disclosed the contrivance.

All

All on a sudden, as he was carrying her on his shoulder quite carelessly, she fired off with a loud report; his horse, which was a colt scarcely broke, being frightened, threw him and ran away.

Being much bruised, he was unable to follow his horse, and limped along towards his gun; he took her up, and began to walk slowly homewards, but appeared to be in a state of great surprize and perturbation.

In a little time she fired again, when recoiling against the side of his head, the cock-pin almost tore off his ear, and she fell a second time on the ground.

He stood some moments in the utmost terror and amazement, before he dared to venture to take her up again; which however he attempted at last, with fear and trembling.

Viewing her with the greatest timidity, care, and attention, and finding the pan shut, he opened it, and seeing it bright, unstained with smoak, and empty, and the whole piece without any uncommon appearance, he said to himself, "Surely "the devil muſt have been in this gun, "but I hope he has got out now; how- "ever, I muſt be careful."

He then walked on once more, holding her out at arm's length from his body, and faſt with both hands; preſently ſhe fired a third time, when his aſtoniſhment is not to be deſcribed: he inſtantly threw her down, and fled behind a tree, terrified beyond expreſſion, and peeping at her from thence.

In this ſituation he continued to watch her, as ſhe then lay upon the ground, until ſhe fired a fourth time; upon that he could contain himſelf no longer, but affrighted, leſt ſhe ſhould turn about and ſhoot him, for he was now well convinced that ſhe was animated, he forgot his bruiſes, and ran away as faſt as his feet could carry him, keeping under cover from tree to tree, with as great caution as ever an Indian retreated from a ſuperior enemy, until he conceived himſelf beyond her reach, when he halted
to

to reſt and breathe, being juſt ready to ſink down with terror and fatigue: at that inſtant ſhe fired again, and, hearing the report, he took to his heels, and never ſtopped any more until he reached his own houſe; where he declared his full aſſurance that the devil, or ſomething worſe, had fixed his head quarters in the fowling-piece.

After he got home, he related to his wife, and to all his neighbours, a moſt lamentable tale of his atchievements and feats of prowefs, in an engagement with the devil; embelliſhed with many extraordinary and fictitious exploits in ſuperabundance.

But the fright, and the fall from his horſe, occaſioned him a ſevere illneſs, which indeed had like to have put his grand antagoniſt in poſſeſſion of him as well as of his gun.

After his recovery he could never be prevailed on to touch that fowling-piece, although he was made acquainted with the ſtratagem that had been impoſed on him;

him; and he was so ridiculed and laughed at by every one, that for a long time he did not venture to show his face in public.

This was the only act of retaliation I inflicted upon this fellow, in return for a multitude of ridiculous silly mischiefs, and stupid foolish tricks, or jokes (as he called them), which he was (before this one retorted on himself) perpetually playing off upon me, and every person he happened to fall in company with.

There was a rich planter's daughter, of her own accord, undertook to polish me (as she was pleased to term it); this was with the approbation of her parents and friends, and certainly she honoured me with every attention, instruction, and kindness.

Indeed, if presents could have rendered me polite, I must have soon become one of the most polished youths in their country; for every present she received from the young gentlemen in the vicinity (which indeed was not a few, the girl being exceedingly handsome), she

insisted

insisted on my accepting, so that at last I knew not what to do with them.

Whilst I remained at this place I met with a very singular occurrence: having purchased a beautiful Chickasaw horse, named so from a nation of Indians who are very careful in preserving a fine breed of Spanish horses they have long possessed, unmixed with any other; the first day that I rode him, he was seized with a violent convulsion fit; the second day with another; the third day he was affected in the same manner, while at grafs in the pasture; the fourth day he was taken in a manner still more extraordinary, his mouth was drawn up over his back, and he began to move on straight forwards, in a direct line, with great speed and force, beating down fences, going over the trunks of fallen trees, and every obstruction in his way; in this manner he rushed on into woods, far distant from settlements, and was followed for seven miles, but being then lost sight of, he was never seen or heard of more.

CHAP.

CHAP. XVIII.

Woods. Glades, or Savannahs. Licks. Hunters. Wild Horses. Peculiar Sentiments of an European, on his Arrival in America.

HERE, during my flow recovery from this dangerous indisposition, I began to accustom myself to walk, or ride, little distances alone in the woods. When I first attempted it, I was sure to get bewildered and lost, every time; which indeed one cannot avoid, until habituated to attend to the sun, the trees, and the water-courses. But it requires the experience of several years, to become a good and experienced wood's-man.

I observed here, in different places in the woods, some considerable glades, savannahs, or meadows. These are natural openings, of a few acres in extent, quite destitute of timber, not a tree, nor even the vestige of one, to be perceived in them;

but

but the ground therein is always covered with abundance of excellent long grafs.

Such meadows are generally to be found near the head fpring, or fource of fmall branches of running water, and are as uncommon in America, as an equal extent of natural woods, and large, ftately, lofty trees are in Europe.

Throughout this inland country, one frequently hears of places called Licks; which appellation, being unintellgible to any but the inhabitants, I fhall embrace this opportunity to explain.

Licks are particular places, moft commonly on the banks of rivers, or creeks, and fometimes at fpring-heads, where the clay or earth is impregnated with faline particles.

Thefe places are frequented by deer, elks, buffaloes, horned cattle, and horfes, which daily refort to them, to lick the earth or clay with their tongues; this they perform with a peculiar relifh and gout, and appear to take great delight therein, coming there, for that purpofe, from the diftance of many miles around.

There

There is likewife another kind of licks here befides. Thefe are alfo on the banks of rivers, lakes, ftreams of water, or large ravines and chafms, and confift of chalk, or calcarious earth, of a teftaceous quality, which is greedily licked up and confumed by all thofe different animals I have already mentioned in the defcription of the former of thefe places.

To the ufe of this latter kind they are prompted by nature and inftinct, for falutary and medicinal purpofes, to correct the acidity of the fuper-abundant vegetative juices accumulated in the ftomach, which would otherwife occafion fevere gripings, ftrictures of the bowels, and many other painful diforders.

All thefe licks are generally frequented by hunters with their rifles, at the dawn of day, or on bright moon-fhine nights, who, by this means, feldom fail of killing fome of the deer, elks, or buffaloes, that refort to them at fuch private times, for the greater fecurity.

These places, however, are only to be found or heard of in the back country, and are generally very confiderable diftances afunder, fome ten, twenty, and thirty miles.

All the inhabitants throughout America, that are diftant from the fea, or faltwater, give their cattle and horfes falt, fometimes once, fometimes twice a week; which is not only to promote their increafe of flefh, but to render them gentle and tame, and to allure them to come often to their owner's plantations; elfe, in the mild fouthern climate, where there is no occafion to provide a ftock of provender for them againft the winter, they would otherwife run wild, and roam far beyond the reach of their proprietors, through this immenfe and unbounded foreft.

Indeed, notwithftanding every precaution, very great numbers of black cattle, horfes, and hogs actually do fo daily, and run at large, entirely wild, without any

any other proprietors than those of the ground they happen to be found upon.

In some parts, each person, in possession of a plantation, has what is called a right in the woods; by which he is entitled to the property of a certain proportion of the live stock that runs wild, such as I just described.

This right they dispose of, and transfer from party to party, in the same manner as affixed property.

And when they want to catch some colts, to render them tame and serviceable, it is an undertaking of no small difficulty to accomplish.

Throughout the middle and back settlements of America, there is no other criterion to ascertain the property of black cattle, sheep, and hogs, but ear-marks alone; and of horses, than brands with red hot irons, and ear-marks also.

Each person's mark differs from another; and they are all severally recorded by the clerk of the county-courts wherein they reside.

This

This is supported by the authority of the legiflature, who have decreed it felony to alter or deface thofe marks or infignia of property.

There is an obfervation very remarkable, which occurred to me, and as I fuppofe to every European on his arrival in America, but I prefume never thought on by any native. It is an idea of reftraint, or a want of free open air, and an extenfion of view, occafioned by the appearance of confinement, and the perfpective being always bounded by the furrounding woods, which perpetually limit the fight within narrower compafs than the mind requires; befides an univerfal gloomy fhade, rendered difmal by the intermixing branches of the lofty trees, which over-fpread the whole country, and the fun never pervades.

This occafioned a fenfation rather painful to me for a confiderable time, which, however, gradually wore off, until I could only juft recollect the idea.

I acknowledge indeed never to have heard this obfervation mentioned by any one whomfoever; but as it ftruck me moſt forcibly, I have therefore every reafon to believe that others have likewife perceived, at firſt, the fame kind of fenfations, if they began to travel foon after their arrival in this part of America.

CHAP.

CHAP. XIX.

Appearance of the Country. Diseases of the Climate. Snakes. Game. Raccoons. Description of the Opposum. Beer made of Persimmons. Cheapness of Land. Delightful Climate. Stanzas written in Solitude.

THE face of the country, ever since I left Mr. Eaton's, has been gradually swelling more and more into hills and dales, which are here called bottoms, as I advanced westward; and the land is likewise more mixed with stones, which also continue to increase in magnitude.

The soil is a composition of reddish clay and loam, strong and fertile; the woods less intermingled with pines, and more with oak and hickory; and the water every where excellent, running in vast multitudes of beautiful clear streams.

The country and climate is in general healthy, the low grounds of the rivers alone otherwise, particularly those of the Roanoak, occasioned by exhalations arising from the damp soil, stagnated waters, and by the putrefcence of the air, whofe free circulation is prevented, in fuch fituations, by lofty thick woods, impervious to the brighteft beams of the fun, under which a difmal gloom and infalubrious moifture eternally reigns.

The inhabitants of thefe places, and their neareft vicinity, are fubject to obftinate intermittents; thefe, and bilious complaints, being the chief and moft prevailing endemial difeafes throughout this country.

There are likewife great numbers of all kinds of ferpents in thefe fituations, particularly that moft poifonous and dreadful of all, the rattle-fnake; and the more filent and dangerous moccoffons alfo abound, efpecially in and near the fwamps, guts, and rivers, but are not met with fo frequently.

Game is very plenty here, particularly deer, beavers, otters, raccoons, and that very extraordinary animal the oppoffum, the female of which has a double, or falfe belly: within it the young ones

grow

grow to the teats, like fruit to the ſtalk, and drop off at a certain period.

After ſhe has brought forth her young, during the ſeaſon of their infancy, whenever they perceive danger nigh, they all run into the mother's bag, or falſe belly, for ſecurity and refuge.

Both theſe and the raccoons are uſed for food, generally barbicued, or roaſted, and their fleſh is not unpleaſant.

There are alſo ſome wolves, and multitudes of foxes, wild turkies very large fat and fine, wild-geeſe, ducks, and ſquirrels innumerable, which make moſt excellent ſoup; alſo wood-peckers and jays of ſeveral different kinds; beſides a vaſt variety of other animals, birds, beaſts, &c. too many even to enumerate.

Great numbers of trees in the woods, eſpecially in the low grounds, are covered with vines, and bend under the weight of the ripe grapes, which are ſuſpended in accumulated multitudes of large and delicious cluſters.

There is also a remarkable fruit named the persimmon, growing wild, about as large as the biggest Orleans plum, of a bright scarlet colour, with four or five very hard seeds in each, nearly of the size and shape of those of tamarinds, and the pulp of the fruit, when perfectly ripe, is of a sharp, but luscious sweetness.

As other fruits are ripened by the sun, so the persimmon is by the frost in conjunction with it; for although beautiful and tempting to the eye, they cannot be eaten, and scarcely even tasted, before they are maturated, or meliorated, by several sharp frosts, previous to which they are austere, rough, and astringent, to a greater degree than any other vegetative substance, or production, whatsoever.

All animals are excessively fond of this fruit, particularly the oppossums and raccoons, who are generally found on, or near the persimmon-trees. These trees are as large as oaks, elms, or ash, and

are

are diftinctly divided into male and female, the male never bearing fruit.

In fome places, where apples and cyder are fcarce, the inhabitants gather the perfimmons, after they are perfectly ripe, knead them into a kind of dough, or pafte, with wheat bran, which they form into loaves, and bake in ovens: of thefe they brew a fermented liquor, which is called perfimmon beer. This ferves for their common drink, and is tolerably pleafant and wholefome. It is fometimes, though rarely, diftilled into brandy.

Thefe trees grow chiefly in or near about the edges of glades, favannahs, and in old fields, as they term fuch places where the timber has been cut down, the land worn out, impoverifhed, or tired with culture, and young trees have not fprung up; for the perfimmon is found to thrive in the pooreft foil, almoft as well as in the moft fertile.

Throughout this back country, there are fo many rich and valuable tracts of land frequently to be difpofed of, for considerations infinitely inferior to their real worth, that a man of reflection, even a traveller, cannot always withstand the temptation.

Here I have evinced the truth of this observation for the second time, having made a purchase of a survey, containing four hundred and fifty acres of excellent land, adjoining Flat river, with a cleared plantation, and a house upon it, for only one hundred pounds sterling.

The first purchase I made was on the banks of the Roanoak, nine miles above Eaton's ferry; it consisted of five hundred and fifty acres, of which about one hundred was in Virginia, mostly low grounds, and the rest in North Carolina, the dividing frontier line interfecting the land. On this there is a plantation, houses, orchards, &c. and a public ferry.

The small part of this tract that lies in Virginia cost me two hundred pounds, although I gave but fifty pounds more for all the rest of the survey that is on the

North Carolina fide of the frontier line, being four hundred and fifty acres.

On this plantation I fettled an overfeer, with a few negroes, and ftock; and committed the whole to the care of my friend, Mr. Alexander, with whom I regularly correfponded.

But with this laft purchafe I was not fo well fatisfied, for when I reflected on the fituation of it, I found it muft be an incumbrance, being fo far inland, and fo far diftant from navigation, that there was but a flender profpect of my reaping any benefit thereby.

This confideration induced me to offer it again for fale, and in the difpofal thereof, I was more fortunate than I had any reafon to apprehend, having fold it for fifty pounds more than it coft me, to a planter, who had juft removed out to this place with his family, from the interior part of Virginia, and intended to make fome more purchafes of adjacent tracts that were quite contiguous to this, and thereby, very opportunely to me, enhanced its value.

The

The winter, if you may call so the finest time of the year, is in this part of the continent more pleasant and agreeable than can be conceived ; neither so hot as to incommode, nor so cold as to displease ; but is constantly a series of the most delightful weather imaginable : ever clear, bright, and serene, the face of nature is perpetually smiling.

As a specimen of the sentiments which this lonesome, recluse situation inspires, the following stanzas, or ode, may not be unacceptable, which claim no farther merit than evincing the natural bias of the human mind to philanthropy and benevolence, when detached from the general intercourse of polished society, and divested of the disguise and incumbrances of modern company and refinement.

It was addressed to Robert Alexander, esq. colonel of the militia of the county of Mecklenburg, in Virginia, the gentleman whom I have already mentioned.

STANZAS;
Or, an ODE to a FRIEND.

I.

Whilſt my friend is improving his fortune and mind,
   On the banks of the rapid Roanoak;
Here to ſilence and ſolitude am I confin'd,
   Like a bird juſt eſcap'd from the hawk*.

II.

While merchants are ſcheming and toiling for gains,
   Uſing means that are honeſt, or vile;
Whilſt narrow-ſoul'd miſers are racking their brains,
   To heap up more gold, and more guile.

III.

Whilſt orators proſtitute talents for fee,
   And juſtice gives way to the caſh;
Whilſt the virtuous, the poor are reſpected by me,
   And rich raſcals ſmart under my laſh.

IV.

While doctors ſell health, by the grain, in retail,
   And barter off death by the lump;
Whilſt int'reſt and power againſt merit prevail,
   And honour's lopt low to the ſtump.

---

* The author being then juſt recovering from a moſt ſevere illneſs.

V.

In obscurity still 'tis my wish to remain,
    Since neglected, forsaken, retir'd;
For riches and splendour, with guile, I disdain,
    Nor by me are high titles desir'd.

VI.

Contentment alone do I covet in life,
    And friendship with you to enjoy;
This adds to our pleasure, and banishes strife,
    And wisely our days we'll employ.

VII.

Reviewing past time, 'tis with rapture we find,
    That at length we've discover'd the right,
Rude, noisy enjoyments expel'd from our mind,
    Each scene now serene is, and bright.

VIII.

Our associates in former tumultuous life,
    With grief, we see rushing along;
Contending, with eager exertion and strife,
    To excel in the culpable throng.

IX.

Let the Muse their deformities glaringly show,
    And Vice in her colours display;
Awak'ning reflection will urge them to know,
    They, like butterflies, blaze but a day.

X.

In all the gay flutter of fashion and dress,
  They approach me,—expecting my praise;
Since, like them, abandon'd to ev'ry excess.—
  Let them listen, with heed, to my lays.

XI.

" For once then to truth and good-humour descend,
  " Nor wax thus ill-natur'dly warm;
" But bear with the cordial advice of a friend
  " Who can blush for himself, and reform.

XII.

" Too long, my dear Sirs, have you madly deny'd
  " A rational use to your eyes;
" And look'd on those actions with envy and pride,
  " Which reflection must hate and despise,

XIII.

" In praise of the fatal excesses of wine,
  " Disdain to be seen with a pen;
" Nor boast of being rais'd into something divine,
  " When debas'd greatly lower than men.

XIV.

" Where murder for honour is shamefully drest,
  " O never attempt to defend;
" Nor plunge the fell sword, for a casual jest,
  " In the breast of your worthiest friend.

XV.

"To a laugh never martyr an innocent name,
"'Tis a malice most cruelly cool;
"Nor plunge the soft virgin in anguish and shame,
"For the loudest applause of a fool.

XVI.

"When fatally fond the sweet victim is grown,
"In pity, in justice, forbear;
"And think that a sister, or child of your own,
"May be drawn to disgrace and despair.

XVII.

"But let merit, where'er it may chance to engage,
"Oblige you to praise and protect;
"And the silver-white ringlets of reverend age,
"Still meet with a decent respect.

XVIII.

"Such conduct will add to your happiness more
"Than all your mistaken pursuits;
"Give zest to your pleasures, and weight to your store,
"Distinguishing reason from brutes."

CHAP. XX.

*Newfo-River. Hillsborough. Strong Post. Haw
Fields. Singular Phenomenon. Accounted for.*

THE last two considerable streams of water that I crossed on my way to this place, Fishing-creek and Tar-river, receiving several inferior creeks and branches in their course, from a tolerable large river, which passing by Tarburg, falls into the immense body of water, that is known by the appellation of Pamplico sound, at Bath town, after a course of about an hundred and fifty miles, in a direct line, from the source.

It was in February when I left this place, and again proceeded on my journey.

At the end of two miles, I crossed Flat river, and in two miles farther, Little river; these, with another river (the Eno) within a couple of miles more, meet some small distance below, and form the river Newse.

Each of these small rivers, is larger than the Thames at Richmond, and the Newse is not much inferior to the Roanoak.

After

After a courſe of more than three hundred miles, it empties itſelf in Pamplico ſound, about thirty miles below the town of Newbern, which is ſometimes called, and lately eſtabliſhed as the capital of North-Carolina.

This town is ſituated in a very beautiful ſpot, on the banks of the Newſe, at the confluence of a pretty ſtream, named Trent river.

After a ride of twenty-two miles, I arrived at Hillſborough, where I dined and paſſed the reſt of the day.

This is the third appellation this town has already been honoured with ſince it was erected, being firſt named Corben-town, next Childſburg, now Hillſborough; all in leſs than thirty years.

It is alſo the capital of a diſtrict, and the county-town of Orange.

Hillſborough is a healthy ſpot, enjoys a good ſhare of commerce for an inland town, and is in a very promiſing ſtate of improvement.

The land, for some distance around Hillsborough, consists of a mixture of loam and strong red clay of so bright a colour that white horses and cattle, soon after they are brought there, become in appearance a fine scarlet.

In the vicinity of Hillsborough, and to the westward of it, there are a great many very fine farms, and a number of excellent mills.

The inhabitants are chiefly natives of Ireland and Germany, but of the very lowest and most ignorant class, who export large quantities of exceeding good butter and flour, in waggons, to Halifax, Petersburg, &c. besides multitudes of fat cattle, beeves, and hogs.

There is a very steep and high hill, or small mountain, with two summits of an equal height, on the south-west of Hillsborough, which arises abruptly in the middle of an extensive plain, and commands the whole country for a great distance around.

This might easily be rendered a very strong post, by works thrown up on the summits, which are near enough to cover and support each other, and so situated, as the communication between them could not be interrupted. The flanks and rear likewise would be strengthened by the river Eno, which runs at the base of this mountain, and washes two sides of it.

The staple produce of all this country being provisions of every kind, a fortified post in this place, would thereby be enabled to subsist and maintain itself in every necessary supply, excepting arms and ammunition, and might be defended, by a small force, against a very considerable and superior army.

Almost every man in this country has been the fabricator of his own fortune, and many of them are very opulent.

Some have obtained their riches by commerce, others by the practice of the law, which in this province is peculiarly lucrative, and extremely oppressive; but most of them

them have acquired their poffeffions by cropping, farming, and induftry.

I dined next day, by invitation, at the houfe of Mr. Frank Nafh.

[Since then it has happened, in the viciffitudes of fortune, that Mr. Nafh and the author were engaged in battle on different fides; Mr. Nafh as a General in the American army, and the author a Captain in the Britifh, at the action of German-Town, near Philadelphia, where Mr. Nafh received his mortal wound.]

Here, at Mr. Nafh's, I happened to meet a Mr. Mabin (a native of Ireland) who very kindly infifted on my accompanying him to his feat on Haw river, adjoining the Haw fields, to fpend fome weeks there.

Having a great defire to view the Haw fields, a place I had heard much about, I went along with him to his plantation, which is about an eafy day's ride, weft of Hillfborough.

Mr. Mabin's farm is very valuable and extensive, but not particularly remarkable.

I rode several times over the Haw fields, but could not perceive any thing in them extraordinary.

They consist partly of wide savannahs, or glades, and partly of large fields overgrown with shrubs, brush, and low under-wood, entirely destitute of heavy timber. But there appears many vestiges of trees, which in all probability have been blown down by a hurricane, and the young shoots afterwards choked by the extreme thickness of the low bushes, and scrubby underwood. This I have also observed to be the case in many other places besides.

From the effect of these most violent and tremendous hurricanes and tornadoes, which being sometimes partial, frequently move in strange fantastic directions, and from the irresistible force of the wind, and the vast deluges and innundations of water that generally accompany them, all the appearances may be readily
ac-

accounted for in a common and natural way, which, however, have lately given fcope to an ingenious, celebrated, and elegant author's (Dr. Dunbar) and others of lefs note (Mr. Carver, &c.) vague imaginations; hazarding their fanciful and wild conjectures of fome of thefe being veftiges of military works, erected many ages paft, by a people *then* converfant in that fcience; but whofe defcendants, *by the mere dint of practice*, (for war and hunting appear from the moft early period of time to have been the fole ftudy and occupation of their lives,) and by fome other equally abfurd and unaccountable tranfitions, have thereby forgotten, and, *at this day*, have loft every trace thereof.

Indeed it muft be confeffed, that the elephant's bones, or thofe of fome other unknown animal of vaft magnitude, found on the banks of the river Ohio, the antique fculptures in the Delaware's country, on the north-weft fide of that amazing river, the fhells and marine fubftances in the Alegany mountains, together with many other ſtrange appearances and ſingular phenomena, ſo frequently to be met with throughout this moſt extenſive continent, diſplay a fertile field for a creative, fanciful genius to explore, and may give riſe to the moſt novel, elegant, and beautiful flights of imagination, and the brighteſt, moſt ingenious, and ſplendid embelliſhments of fiction.

However, I have reaſon to believe, that ſome of the Haw fields have been cleared of woods by the Indians, in ages paſt, who were undoubtedly ſettled here; many inſignia, and veſtiges of the remains of their towns, ſtill remaining.

CHAP.

CHAP. XXI.

Haw river. Deep river. Cape Fear river. Carroway mountains. Grand and elegant Perspective. Bad Accommodations. Unsuitable to an Epicure, or a Petit Maitre.

HAVING it in speculation to visit Henderson's settlement on Kentucky, I mentioned my intention to Mr. Mabin, who appeared very strenuous in dissuading me from undertaking such an enterprize at present, on account of the misunderstanding and disturbances now subsisting between the Indians and the Whites.

He informed me of a report, that even Henderson's whole settlement was either exterminated, or in imminent danger of being so.

For this reason, I concluded to postpone this arduous undertaking, until such time as more certain and favourable intelligence of their situation in the settlement should arrive, and a better prospect of reaching it without molestation.

On the third evening after I came here, a gentleman, named Frohawk, called at Mr. Mabin's, on his return to Salisbury, where he resided.

As he tarried all night, we had much conversation, and from his accounts of the Catawba Indians, my curiosity was strongly excited to visit their nation, which was only about an hundred miles beyond the town of Salisbury.

Accordingly, having expressed my desire and intention to Mr. Frohawk, he was so obliging as to propose to conduct and accompany me; an opportunity and eligible offer, which I with great satisfaction embraced, and set out along with him next morning.

The road we travelled in is named the Great Trading Path, and leads through Hillsborough, Salisbury, &c. to the Catawba towns, and from thence to the Cherokee nation of Indians, a considerable distance westward.

We forded the Haw river, which is there about twice as broad as the Thames at Putney, and within a few miles farther, in the like manner, we crossed Reedy river, another branch of the same stream, and as large.

We dined just by a Quaker's meetinghouse, and in the afternoon crossed Deep river, at a ford. This is also about twice as wide as the Thames at Putney, and joins the Haw river some distance below, after washing the base of the north-east side of a ridge or chain of high hills, named the Carroway mountains.

The Haw is then a large river, and runs through the settlement and town of Cross creek, which is chiefly inhabited by Scots emigrants from the western Highlands and the Hebrides*: it then assumes a new appellation, being called the Northwest, or Cape Fear river, and passing by the town of Wilmington, which has been frequently considered as the metropolis of

---

* For an account of the unhappy fate of this loyal and patriotic settlement, on account of their attachment to their King and Country, see Chap. xxxi.

North-Carolina, on the north-eaft, and Brunfwick, which is a little lower on the weftern bank of the river, it falls into the Atlantic ocean at Cape Fear, after a courfe of more than three hundred miles from the fource.

We lodged that night at an inn or ordinary, as it is called here, at the foot of the Carroway mountains, which we had frequently had a glimpfe of, during this day's ride.

We purfued our journey early on the following morning, which was extremely pleafant and fine; and when we arrived at the fummit of the mountain, the fun juft began to verge above the horizon.

Here I alighted, and indulged myfelf in gazing with great delight on the wild and extenfive profpect around me.

On the north-eaft I beheld the mountains at Hillfborough, diftant above fifty miles; on the fouth-weft, the mountains near Salifbury; and on the weft, Tryon mountains; with the wide extended foreft below, embrowned with thick woods, and
inter-

interfected with dark, winding, narrow chafms, which marked out the courfe of the different mighty ftreams that meandered through this enormous vale; thinly interfperfed on the banks of which, the farms and plantations appeared like as many infignificant fpots, that, while they pointed out the induftry, ferved alfo to expofe the littlenefs of man.

On this fpot I could with pleafure have paffed the day, had not a craving, keen appetite reminded us, that there are more gratifications neceffary for our fupport, than feafting our eyes; fo we defcended the mountain, and purfued our journey.

It was fortunate for me, that at this time, my conftitution, health, and tafte, enabled me to fubfift on any kind of food, without repining, and with fufficient fatisfaction, however coarfe or unufual it might be. For this is not an enterprife for an epicure, or a petit maître: the apprehenfions of perifhing with hunger and want, would as effectually deter the one from fuch an undertaking, as the dread of abfolutely expiring with fatigue and hardfhips, would the other; the fare and accommodations a traveller meets with throughout this country, being very indifferent indeed, even at beft, and generally miferable and wretched beyond defcription, excepting at warm or opulent planters houfes, where there is always a profufion of every thing, but in the coarfeft and plaineft ftyle.

The greater number of thofe who travel through this country, have acquaintances among the inhabitants, at whofe houfes they generally put up every night, and feldom call at ordinaries.

Thofe that drive and accompany waggons on a journey, fleep in the woods every night under a tree, upon dry leaves on the ground, with their feet towards a large fire, which they make by the road fide, wherever night happens to overtake them, and are covered only with a blanket. Their horfes are turned loofe in the woods, only with leather fpancills or fet-
ters

ters on two of their legs, and each with a bell faſtened by a collar round his neck, by which they are readily found in the morning. Proviſions and provender, both for men and horſes, are carried along with them, in the waggon, ſufficient for the whole journey.

Even theſe advantages, trifling as they may appear, a traveller on horſeback is deſtitute of, and is obliged to truſt to Providence, and the country through which he paſſes, for accommodation and ſubſiſtence; both of which are not always to be met with, and even when they are, are ſeldom as good, never better than the waggoners.

CHAP.

CHAP. XXII.

Yadkin River. Salisbury. Beautiful Perspective. Tryon Mountain. Brushy Mountains. The King Mountain distinguished for the unhappy Fate of the gallant Major Ferguson.

LATE in the afternoon we crossed the river Yadkin, at a ford, six or seven miles beyond which is the town of Salisbury, where we arrived that evening, being about one hundred and twenty miles west-south-west from Hillsborough.

The Yadkin is a very large stream of water, at least three times as wide as the Thames at Putney: it runs through a rich and extensive country, enters South Carolina, passing through the Chawraws, having a vast body of low grounds and rich rice and indigo lands on each side, before which it assumes the name of Great Peedee, and falls into the Atlantic Ocean a few miles below George-Town, which stands on the west side of a bay a bay named Winyaw, formed within the mouth of this river, receiving a great many inferior ſtreams in its courſe, which is remarkably crooked, being above five hundred miles along with its meanders, and more than four hundred miles, in a direct line, from its ſource.

Saliſbury is the capital of a diſtrict, and is the county town of Roan: it is ſituated on a ſmall creek that runs into the Yadkin on the ſouth-weſt ſide.

This town is larger than Hillſborough, and leſs than Halifax; but does not ſhare an equal degree of commerce with the leaſt of them.

The trade from Saliſbury is pretty exactly divided between the towns on James River in Virginia, and Charles Town in South Carolina.

There is a beautiful romantic mountain a few miles due ſouth from Saliſbury, which being ſeen from the town produces a very fine effect, as the Carroway mountains do alſo, the tops of which are likewiſe to be perceived.

I went

I went to the summit of this delightful mountain, on the brow nearest to the town, and from thence beheld a perspective, beautiful, extensive, and grand, as I always do such a scene, with superior pleasure.

On the north-east I observed the Carroway mountains; on the north-west, at fifty miles distance, the Brushy Mountains, the Montague Hills, and the King's Mountain on the west.

[It was on this mountain that gallant officer and excellent partizan, Major Ferguson, of the British army, and his whole detachment, were cut off, and killed by a vast superiority of the rebels, in November 1780; by which misfortune this place has unhappily become distinguished.]

On the south and east I beheld an unbounded plain; and the whole an immense forest, without limits, interspersed with vast water-courses, and thinly spotted with settlements.

Mr.

Mr. Frohawk being prevented by an unforeseen accident from accompanying me to the Catawba nation, I set out alone, and after a fatiguing ride of sixty miles, arrived at a little town, named Charlottesburg, at night; having forded several water-courses during the day, which form Rocky River, a branch of the Yadkin.

Charlottesburg is an inconsiderable place, and in England would not be thought deserving of even the name of a village. It stands upon a creek that runs into the Catawba River, is not a county town, and its trade and share of commerce is very insignificant.

During this day's ride, I observed that the settlements are fewer, the plantations smaller, and the land, in appearance, less fertile, than on the other side of Salisbury.

CHAP. XXIII.

Blazed Path. Origin and Use thereof. Description of a Back Wood's Rifleman. His strange Dress and peculiar Sentiments..

THROUGHOUT all this country, and in every back settlement in America, the roads and paths are first marked out by blazes on the trees, cut alternately on each side of the way, every thirty or forty yards: these are renewed every time the roads are repaired.

A blaze is a large chip sliced off the side of a tree with an axe; it is above twelve inches in length, cut through the bark and some of the sap wood, and by its white appearance, and brightness, when fresh made, serves to direct the way in the night as well as in the day.

The miles are chiefly computed, and are ascertained by notches chopped in the nearest tree; a notch for every mile.

The first blazed paths originated in this manner: when any person went from one

one place to another through the woods, where it would have been difficult, if not impoffible, to return upon his track, he fell upon this method of blazing each fide of the trees, at certain diftances, as he paffed on, and thereby retraced his way in returning, without the leaft trouble.

The convenience and fimplicity of this mode has rendered it univerfal throughout the whole back country.

It became the more readily adopted, as all who travel beyond the roads and beaten tracks, always have tomahawks in their belts; which, in fuch fituations and circumftances, are more useful than any thing, except the rifle-barreled firelocks; both of which all the male inhabitants habituate themfelves conftantly to carry along with them every where.

Their whole drefs is alfo very fingular, and not very materially different from that of the Indians; being a hunting fhirt, fomewhat refembling a waggoner's frock, ornamented with a great many fringes, tied round the middle with a broad belt, much decorated alfo, in which is faftened a tomahawk, an inftrument that ferves every purpofe of defence and convenience; being a hammer at one fide and a fharp hatchet at the other; the fhot bag and powder-horn, carved with a variety of whimfical figures and devices, hang from their necks over one fhoulder; and on their heads a flapped hat, of a reddifh hue, proceeding from the intenfely hot beams of the fun.

Sometimes they wear leather breeches; made of Indian dreffed elk, or deer fkins, but more frequently thin trowfers.

On their legs they have Indian boots, or leggings, made of coarfe woollen cloth, that either are wrapped round loofely and tied with garters, or are laced upon the outfide, and always come better than half way up the thigh: thefe are a great defence and prefervative, not only againft the bite of ferpents and poifonous infects, but likewife againft the fcratches of thorns, briars, fcrubby bufhes, and under-

underwood, with which this whole country is infested and overspread.

On their feet they sometimes wear pumps of their own manufacture, but generally Indian moccossons, of their own construction also, which are made of strong elk's, or buck's skin, dressed soft as for gloves or breeches, drawn together in regular plaits over the toe, and lacing from thence round to the fore part of the middle of the ancle, without a seam in them, yet fitting close to the feet, and are indeed perfectly easy and pliant.

Thus habited and accoutered, with his rifle upon his shoulder, or in his hand, a back-wood's man is completely equipped for visiting, courtship, travel, hunting, or war.

And according to the number and variety of the fringes on his hunting shirt, and the decorations on his powder-horn, belt, and rifle, he estimates his finery, and absolutely conceives himself of equal consequence, more civilized, polite, and more elegantly dressed than the most brilliant peer at St. James's, in a splendid and expensive birth-day suit, of the first fashion and taste, and most costly materials.

Their hunting, or rifle shirts, they have also died in variety of colours, some yellow, others red, some brown, and many wear them quite white.

Such sentiments as those I have just exposed to notice, are neither so ridiculous nor surprising, when the circumstances are considered with due attention, that prompt the back-wood's American to such a train of thinking, and in which light it is, that he feels his own consequence, for he finds all his resources in himself.

Thus attired and accoutered, as already described, set him in the midst of a boundless forest, a thousand miles from an inhabitant, he is by no means at a loss, nor in the smallest degree dismayed.

With his rifle he procures his subsistence; with his tomahawk he erects his

shelter,

shelter, his wigwam, his house, or whatever habitation he may chuse to reside in; he drinks at the cryftal spring, or the neareft brook; his wants are all easily supplied, he is contented, he is happy. For felicity, beyond a doubt, confifts, in a great measure, in the attainment and gratification of our desires, and the accomplishment of the utmoft bounds of our wishes.

This digreffion, which I thought neceffary to imprefs an idea of the fingular appearance and sentiments of these men, for that reason, I am hopeful, will be excused; and for which, I flatter myself, this will be deemed a sufficient apology.

CHAP. XXIV.

Catawba Indians. The King. Once a powerful Nation. Customs. Depopulation. Causes thereof. Manner of Life. Abortions of the young Women.

ON the morning following I pursued my journey to the Catawba towns, which are between thirty and forty miles distant from Charlottesburg.

Having hired a person at Charlottesburg, who was well acquainted in the nation, and conversant in their language and customs, to serve as my guide, and interpreter, if there should be occasion, we arrived at the nation that evening.

Our horses were turned out loose, and we lodged in a wigwam belonging to a family of these Indians, in which my guide was very intimate.

My bed was a large bear's skin, with a blanket to cover me, and I slept on the ground, before the fire. Being very much fatigued, I rested tolerably well, and in
the

the morning I arofe early, as ufual, and walked out to view the town.

This day I had the honour of being introduced to the king, or chief of the Catawba nation, whofe hard-mouthed Indian appellation I cannot recollect, but his Englifh name was Joe.

He appeared to be a ftrong, ftraight, well-looking, robuft fellow, little or no way diftinguifhable from the reft, otherwife than in the accidental gifts of his perfon; for he feemed to me the likelieft, beft made, and handfomeft man in the nation.

I was not a little furprifed to find that they all fpoke Englifh very intelligibly; and they informed me that they underftand, and pronounce it as well as their own language.

This once numerous, powerful, and even lately very refpectable nation, is now dwindled away almoft to nothing, there being at this time no more than fixty or feventy warriors in the whole, and fuch they are, as would excite the derifion

and

and contempt of the more western savages, for these are in a kind of state of civilization, which the Indians consider as enervating effeminacy, and hold it in the utmost abhorrence.

The Catawbas afford a melancholy example, and striking, but insuperable proof, of the ruin and fatality brought on any Indian nation, by the intemperance and vicinity of the settlements of the whites.

This astonishing havoc and depopulation, which is indeed most alarming, grievous, and awful, and truly painful for humanity to reflect upon, has been occasioned, in a great measure, by the introduction of the small-pox and spirituous liquors.

Their injudicious treatment of that infectious malady, generally renders it fatal, for they make use of hot stimulating medicines to promote a most profuse diaphoresis, in the height of which, whilst reeking with sweat, and dissolving in streams of warm moisture, they rush out

into

into the open air, quite naked, and suddenly plunge into the deepest and coldest stream of running water that can be found, immersing their whole body in the chilling flood.

It may well be supposed, that if their recovery was doubtful before, this renders it totally impossible; and the poor unfortunate victims fall sacrifices to the most wretched ignorance and folly.

The deleterious effects of spirituous liquors are not less notorious and extensive; for these unhappy wretches are one and all perfectly devoted to the immoderate use of them, when to be obtained by any means whatsoever in their power; and an universal inebriation constantly occasions a most dreadful carnage, which all the persuasions and power of the women, invariably exerted for that laudable purpose, is never able to prevent.

Yet after the fatal paroxysm of intoxication has ceased, no revenge is gratified, no resentments are indulged by the
rela-

relations and friends of the murdered, against the survivor.

The brothers, the fathers, the sons of the deceased, are perfectly reconciled to, and in the strictest harmony and friendship with those that perpetrated the sanguinary deed. All unite in exculpating the actors from intentional crime, throwing the whole blame and stigma of evil and guilt on the wicked and pernicious spirits that gave rise to the whole.

Although every one execrates the abominable liquor, and appears to show the deepest contrition for the dreadful scene of which that alone was the sole cause, yet if they can procure as much more the very next night as will completely intoxicate them, they cannot resist the temptation, even if they were assured of as much mischief as before proceeding from it.

The women, therefore, as soon as they discover spirituous liquors in the house, hut, or wigwam, begin immediately to
secrete

secrete and convey away every dangerous weapon and inftrument of death.

The latent effects of thefe are not lefs prejudicial and deftructive to population than thofe more immediate and apparent. For the warrior neglects his hunting; the fquaw neglects her agriculture; the mother neglects her children; ill health and difeafe fucceed, which generally terminate in the final exit of the unhappy victims, by immerfion in the cold bath, while almoft in a ftate of liquefaction by heat and a moft profufe perfpiration.

The decreafe and depopulation of the Indian nations is alfo promoted by another caufe befides thefe, which has contributed as powerfully as either of the former to that fatal purpofe.

It is the frequent abortions of the young unmarried women: for they confider a promifcuous intercourfe between the fexes before marriage as no difgrace, nor does it prevent a girl from obtaining a hufband afterwards; but they are careful to deftroy the fruits of this licentious connection by medicinal simples that promote abortion, in which fatal science they are very expert. It produces this pernicious effect, that such practices in their early youth subject them to miscarriages ever afterwards, and when it happens otherwise, they commonly have not more than two children, very seldom three, during the whole course of their lives.

However, although devotees to incontinence and the Cytherian rites while single, yet after they marry they are remarkable for their fidelity to the objects of their choice, unless they should happen to take a dislike to each other; then they mutually agree on an immediate separation, or divorce, and each party may marry again with any other person, without the smallest censure, or the least idea of impropriety.

It is customary when a white man enters an Indian town, or nation, with intention of residing there for some time, if only a few months, for him to have

have a wigwam, or hut, erected, in which he lives with some young squaw, whom he either courts to his embraces, or receives from her parents as his wife and servant, during the time he may stay among them.

In such cases she is always very faithful and true, and if she should prove pregnant, the child is raised by the nation: but if she be the daughter of one of their chiefs, and the father of the infant be inclined to fix his residence among them, he is presented with a large tract of land, several miles square, in trust for the child; which, as well as himself, is then formally adopted and received into the nation.

CHAP. XXV.

Catawba's vaſt Property. Their Manufactures. Their Naſtineſs.

THE Catawbas are indeed a poor, inoffenſive, inſignificant people, enveloped in filth and naſtineſs of perſon, for no Indian has any idea of cleanneſs.

But they poſſeſs an extenſive and moſt valuable body of rich, fertile land, containing more than one hundred and fifty thouſand acres, which they hold in abſolute property and fee ſimple inheritance.

Should their depopulation continue as rapidly as it has been hitherto, in a very few years this enormous, immenſe eſtate will center in a ſingle family.

However, this eſtate, vaſt and immenſe as it is, is but a poor compenſation for the loſs of a whole province; for this nation formerly poſſeſſed, and were the actual proprietors of the greateſt part of North Carolina.

I am

I am told that there can be no certain determined judgment formed of the manners and appearance of the native, uncivilized, wild, western Indians, from these, who seem indeed, in a great meaſure, to have loſt that martial independent ſpirit, for which that whole race of mankind have been ever diſtinguiſhed, and to be ſinking faſt into degeneracy and a ſtate of ſervility and dependence, inferior even to the moſt indigent of the whites.

The Indian women in general are called *Squaws*, and it is their buſineſs to cultivate the ſoil, as well as perform the common menial domeſtic ſervices; the ſole occupation of the men being war, hunting, fiſhing, fowling, and ſmoaking tobacco.

The only manufacture that I can diſcover among them is that of party-coloured little baſkets, table-mats, made of ſtraw, and chips, or ſplits of different coloured wood; and an ill-formed kind of a half-baked earthen ware.

These insignificant trifles are carried about by the squaws for sale, and are purchased for the most worthless invaluable considerations.

Many of the Catawbas have affixed property of various kinds and descriptions, and some of their hunters dispose of more than one hundred pounds value of deer-skins every year

Nothing can be more simple, submissive, and obliging than the behaviour of every individual I met with in the Catawba nation, male and female: and there was only their habitual nastiness, coarse fare, and rude accommodations that were any wise disgustful to me, during my residence among them.

However, these people seem to enjoy an ample share of the most valuable of all human blessings, the most estimable of all transitory possessions, health, contentment, and felicity; their principal concern proceeding from the apprehensions of the encroachments of the whites, of which all Indians are indeed,
with

United States of America. 195

with great reafon, extremely jealous and watchful. For no extenfion of territory can gratify our infatiable defires, no bounds can limit our perpetual ufurpations, invafions, and inroads on the undoubted and fole property and domain of thefe comparatively defencelefs and innocent race of aboriginal inhabitants.

[For a more particular account of the character and difpofition of the Indians, and of the name, fituation, and ftrength, or number of warriors, of each nation on the continent of North-America, fee Chap. xliii. and xliv.]

CHAP. XXVI.

Catawba River. An uncommon Instance of Penury. Rich Miser. Wretchedness and Misery of his Slaves. Wateree River. Congarees River. Santee River. Their great Extent. Fertility of the Soil.

HAVING, in a few days, sufficiently gratified my curiosity amongst this sinking and degenerating nation, I left the Catawbas, and set out on a journey to a very distinguished place of trade, in South-Carolina, lately entitled Camden, the capital of a district of the same name, formerly called, and still most universally known, by the appellation of the Pine-tree.

Having found my guide, or interpreter, useful to me as a servant, I continued to employ him to attend me, which seemed to afford him great satisfaction, although he was engaged for the small wages of half-a-crown per day for himself and his horse also. However, it must be acknowledged, we always lodged and fared alike.

The dividing line between North and South-Carolina, intersects the Catawba nation.

nation. The principal town, however, is in South Carolina.

We set out from hence in the morning very early, and within the distance of about seven miles, crossed the Catawba river, at a ford just above the confluence of a considerable rivulet that falls into it on the north-east side named Twelve Mile creek, leaving the great road or trading path on our right, that leads west towards the Cherokee country, our course being almost due south a little easterly; and during all this morning's ride hitherto, we have still been upon the territory belonging to the Catawba nation.

The Catawba is a large and rapid river, containing an enormous quantity of water: it is about three hundred and fifty yards wide, and, although fordable, is deep, and runs in a rocky channel with great velocity.

This day we had a dreary ride, and miserable accommodations; having breakfasted on some rice and milk, which it was with much difficulty we could procure,

cure, and we dined wretchedly at an ordinary of the same style, on the banks of a rivulet, named Fishing creek, which we forded, as also Rocky creek, and lodged at night in a house, or rather a hovel, belonging to a Mr. D—, a private and penurious planter.

In this habitation, which had many strong features of indigence, was only one room and one bed, which the proprietor himself occupied, but very benevolently afforded us (indeed with some degree of reluctance) the accommodation of a pallet on the floor; and after our fatiguing ride of more than fifty miles, even this was very acceptable.

However this house, or more properly shelter, appeared to me as another mansion of misery, and strongly recalled to my mind the poor overseer's wretched habitation, where I lodged the first night after I left Petersburg, in Virginia.

This solitary recluse I also considered as a poor, disconsolate, despised overseer, in the employment of some opulent proprietor

prietor wallowing in the wealth and luxuries of Charles-town.

Fully possessed with this idea, which I had imbibed over-night from every penurious appearance, I walked out early in the morning to take a general view of the plantation and agriculture.

After strolling about for a considerable time, without meeting a single person to answer any interrogation, I happened to go into a large barn, where to my astonishment, there were near fifty negroes at work.

I asked them to whom they belonged? They replied, to Mr. D——. Who is Mr. D——? Where does he live?—And to my great surprise, I found it was the poor penurious wretch on whose floor we had lodged, that was proprietor, not only of this estate, but of many other plantations, together with three or four hundred more half-starved negroes besides.

I departed from this place with a mixture of pity and contempt for the miserable wretch, who, possessing such a fortune, was incapable of using it as he ought, for the purposes of benevolence, and the benefit of mankind.

But with my heart penetrated with pain and anguish, I commiserated the fate of those unhappy wretches his slaves, who were not allowed even a sufficiency of the coarsest common necessaries of life, in compensation for the hard labour of their lives, by this griping son of penury, who also endeavoured to avert his ruin, and fulfilled his consistency, by sending us away without breakfast.

After an unpleasant ride of better than twenty-five miles, and crossing the river Wateree (which is a continuance of the Catawba) in a ferry-boat, I arrived at Camden, or the Pine-tree, about noon.

This river, the Catawba, assumes three several appellations, but in different places. The upper part is named the Catawba, the middle is the Wateree, which appellation is continued to it as far as the confluence of the great Congarees river, on its south-west side, from thence it is
called

called the Santee to its mouth at Cape Roman or Carteret.

The Catawba river, from its source in the Apalachian or Alegany mountains in North-Carolina, to the mouth of Santee in the Atlantic ocean on the coaſt of South-Carolina, is nearly ſix hundred miles in length, along with its meanders, and almoſt five hundred miles in a ſtraight line; containing an aſtoniſhing quantity of water. Including the other branches of this river, which alſo fall into the Santee, it paſſes through a country as rich and fertile, and contains on and adjoining its waters as large a quantity of fine land, as any river of its extent in the univerſe.

CHAP.

CHAP. XXVII.

Camden. Lands. Rivers. Infects. Inhabitants. Rice, Indigo. Manure.

CAMDEN is a place of confiderable commerce, and is improving very faft, but I do not think it meriting the pains, fatigue, and trouble, I have taken to fee it, for I can difcover nothing particularly remarkable, either in the town, or in the country around it.

It is about an hundred and fifty miles, in a direct courfe, from Salifbury; but is an hundred and eighty, or near two hundred miles, by the circuitous route I made by the Catawbas, and between one hundred and fixty and an hundred and eighty miles from Charles Town.

There is no hill, fcarcely an eminence near it, excepting Santee hills, about thirty miles to the eaftward, on the fame fide of the river, but at the diftance of feveral miles from the banks, and they

continue

continue in a chain, nearly in the same direction, for thirty or forty miles farther.

Here the land is divided into first and second low grounds, and high lands or barrens.

The first and second low grounds are what is cultivated, and formed into plantations, producing crops of Indian corn, rice, and indigo.

The high or barren land is divided into oak and pine barrens; of which the oak is always the sign of the more fertile soil, for the pine barrens are only pine or fir-trees growing, scattered promiscuously, in a bed of loose, deep sand, which scarcely produces a single blade of verdure, and is excessively fatiguing and troublesome for either horses or men to travel through, every step therein sinking almost to the knee.

In the woods, especially in the low-grounds of all the rivers, creeks and branches of water, vast quantities of reeds spontaneously vegetate, and are in a perpetual state of verdure, affording most excellent

excellent food for cattle and horses, which keep fat upon this provender all the year round; for no provision or forage of any kind is required to be laid in for them against the winter, as during that season they are the fattest.

For here all the inclemency of the weather is in the summer, when the intenseness of the heat, and the scorching rays of the sun, the multitudes of noxious and troublesome flies, and innumerable other pernicious insects, continually exhaust, prey upon, and torment every living creature in the fields and woods, sucking their blood, fretting, and torturing them almost to death; so that at this time of the year, every kind of beast falls away, and becomes miserably poor and lean. For even to mankind, with all his resources and advantages, the heat then becomes intolerable, nor can he find any shelter or defence against the assaults of these flies, insects, and poisonous reptiles, that then infest the whole surface of nature.

The country is throughout one continued plain and foreſt, with the plantations and ſettlements formed only upon the ſides of the rivers and water-courſes. The inhabitants are a feeble race, of a tawney, or yellowiſh hue, and ſallow, cadaverous complexions; but many of the rice and indigo planters in this neighbourhood are very gay and opulent.

Even the Negroes are ſhrivelled, and diminutive in ſize, compared with thoſe in Virginia; nor is their value equal, as I am informed, to theirs by near fifty per cent.

The culture of both rice and indigo is extremely unwholſome, as the former muſt be covered with water, during the greater part of the time of its vegetation; and the putrid exhalations, proceeding from the ſtagnated water, muſt be particularly injurious to health, and occaſion obſtinate intermittents.

The indigo alſo requires a great deal of water in its manufacture, and ſoon becomes rotten and putrid in this ſultry climate: afterwards nothing can be more

offenſive

offensive and infalubrious than it is; yet, in that state of the highest putrescence, they manure their lands with it, spreading it over their fields whilst wet and stinking, which thereby became abominably noisome, and absolutely render the whole surrounding atmosphere, within the influence or contact of the offensive putrid effluvia, extremely deleterious and baneful.

South-Carolina was, for a long time, without a single court of judicature for the distribution of law, justice, or equity, throughout its whole extent, excepting at Charles Town, the metropolis, which was a grievance of very great magnitude to individuals, and really detrimental to the province at large; to palliate which, the jurisdiction of single magistrates was enlarged, and extended. However, it was peculiarly beneficial to the inhabitants of Charles Town, who were in a great measure enriched thereby, as a vast concourse of people from every part of the province, as well as from other governments, were then drawn there perpetually.

But lately, South-Carolina has been divided into fix diftinct diftricts: viz. George Town, Charles Town, Beaufort, Orangefburg, Camden, and Chawraw: at the capital, or chief town of each of which, courts of juftice, common-pleas, quarter-feffions, &c. are eftablifhed, and regularly held. Since that period, the whole country has been confiderably benefited by the meafure, and has flourifhed exceedingly,

In the calculation, made by the Congrefs, of the number of inhabitants in each ftate, South-Carolina is faid to contain two hundred and twenty-five thoufand one hundred and fixteen, of which one fifth part only are Whites. I have good reafon to believe this number to be exaggerated about twenty-five thoufand one hundred and fixteen.

This country has alfo decreafed in population confiderably fince the rebellion, efpecially fince the evacuation of Charles Town, when it is suppofed near ten thoufand inhabitants left the province.

Throughout all this large and valuable province, there are only three fea-ports; the chief of which is Charles Town, with George Town on the north-eaft, and Port Royal on the fouth-weft: the latter has much the beft harbour of the whole, the other two being incumbered with bars at their entrance, which render them inacceffible to large fhips, and difficult to any, efpecially as feveral of thefe banks and quickfands are reported to fluctuate, and frequently change their pofition.

CHAP.

CHAP. XXVIII.

Great Curiosity of the lower Class of Inhabitants. Impertinent Questions. Conjectures of my Guide. Rendered serviceable.

HAVING soon sufficiently gratified my curiosity in Camden and its vicinity, and hearing much conversation again concerning Henderson's settlement on Kentucky, the rout to which being now thought safe, I changed my design of proceeding to Charles-Town, for that of an expedition to the Ohio, which had long been the first object of my wishes; intending to defer visiting Charles-Town, Savannah, Augusta, St. Augustine, &c. until after my return from Kentucky.

Accordingly I set out for Salisbury, by the nearest way, intending to pass through the Moravian towns on my journey from thence to Hillsborough, from which place I proposed to begin my expedition to Henderson's new settlement; these Moravians and their towns having been the only

only objects and places deserving attention, that escaped my observation on my progress southward.

It was about the last of April when I departed from Camden, the heat of the weather was increasing fast, and began to be troublesome: but this was the very best season of the year to enter upon my present hazardous undertaking.

On the third day at noon my guide Clifton took his last farewell of me, being nearly opposite to Charlottesburg, the place of his residence.

Having found him extremely useful and attentive, in return for his services and fidelity, I presented him with a gratuity of eight dollars at parting, over and above his scanty wages, at which the poor fellow was absolutely over-joyed, and, as I have frequently heard since, has resounded my praises, and his gratitude, far and near.

It may not be improper here to observe, how very troublesome and disagreeable the extreme curiosity of the lower class of in-

inhabitants at firſt appears to ſtrangers and travellers.

I was for a long time exceedingly peſtered with the impertinent interrogations of, 'What was my buſineſs? What I ſought after? Where did I intend to ſettle? and What brought me to this country?'

As I always found ſome expedient to evade anſwering theſe queſtions, each reſolved his own in the manner his imaginations and conjectures inclined him to believe, and they were all ſatisfied; but every one was preſſing for me to fix my reſidence in his neighbourhood.

My honeſt guide firſt took it into his head, that I was endeavouring to diſcover a judicious ſituation to commence and extend an European commerce; but finding that I paſſed by and overlooked the moſt excellent ſpots for that purpoſe, and that I took great notice of the face of the country, and of the quality and fertility of the ſoil, and examined into the ſtate, nature, and mode of agriculture, as I paſſed; all theſe,

these, with my avowed intentions, which I had frequently expressed, of visiting Henderson's settlement on Kentucky, induced him at length to alter his first opinion, and form an absolute conclusion, that I was a speculator in lands, sparing neither trouble, expence, nor enquiry to discover the finest land, and best bargains, to make purchases of.

This supposititious report he constantly circulated, and it spread with great celerity to an astonishing extent. However, I never found any injury or prejudice attend me on that account, but rather the reverse, for every person appeared studious to contribute to my amusement and information wherever I went, and by this means I acquired a degree of knowledge, which otherwise could not have been obtained in double the time; and besides I was always beheld in a respectable light.

CHAP.

CHAP. XXIX.

Salisbury. Moravian River. Moravian Towns and Settlement. Peculiar Customs and Police. Women in Common. Flourishing State. Their Manufactures. Produce. Salem. Bethania. Bethabara. Their Situations.

AS I rode easy journies, it was on the fourth day after my departure from Camden that I arrived at Salisbury.

Here I remained but one night, and set out next morning very early for the Moravian towns, which lie almost due north from Salisbury.

I crossed Grant's Creek about four miles from the town, and just above its mouth I crossed the Yadkin, at a very bad ford, about nine or ten miles from Salisbury.

About ten miles farther I forded the Moravian River at its mouth, just above where it enters the Yadkin, and rode along an exceeding bad rough road up the western side of the river, until I arrived at Bethania, which is the most westerly and northerly of all the Moravian towns, being about fifty miles from Salisbury.

It stands upon a water-course named Bethania Creek, which is a considerable branch of the Moravian River.

It was late at night before I arrived. I was extremely fatigued, and departed next morning for Bethabara, which I reached to breakfast, after fording another branch of the Moravian River, about six miles on this side of Bethania.

This town is ten miles from the other; but being informed that Salem was the principal, I immediately proceeded on after breakfast, and arrived there about noon, this place being only about seven miles distant from Bethabara.

This society, sect, or fraternity of the Moravians have every thing in common, and are possessed of a very large and extensive property.

They have a kind of monastic institution in their internal police, and in bringing up and educating the younger of both sexes, who are totally secluded

from

from converfation, or intercourfe, with each other, until marriage; after which a houfe, a portion of land, ftock, and utenfils of every kind, are allotted each couple, and the produce of their labour and induftry is depofited in the common ftock.

From their infancy they are inftructed in every branch of ufeful and common literature, as well as in mechanical knowledge and labour, which even then is converted to beneficial and profitable purpofes, for the emolument of the community at large.

But their peculiar uniformity in drefs, and the long beards of the men of that particular fect of them, commonly called Dunkards, have a very fingular, ftriking, and uncouth appearance.

The children are feparated from their parents during their earlieft infancy, and are brought up altogether, each fect diftinct from the other, in a kind of feminaries, as belonging only to the whole fociety, to whom collectively a parental affection is by this means affiduoufly inculcated, cherished, and established; and all perfonal attachments and paternal love and regard are as diligently checked, difcouraged, diminished, and, in a great degree, annihilated.

It is faid that parents actually cannot diftinguish their own offspring from others; and that the children alfo as foon forget every trace by which they might recognize their parents: as they are feparated during the earlieft ftage of infancy, this is readily accomplished and eafily accounted for.

It is alfo reported that thofe members of the fociety who have arrived at years of maturity, particularly the rulers or elders, enjoy their women in common, fo that the parents on one fide are difficult to be afcertained. This circumftance, however, though much and almoft univerfally credited, they themfelves abfolutely deny; and I fhall not undertake to pronounce a decifion, or even an opinion, one way or the other.

The

The Moravians have many excellent and very valuable farms, on which they make large quantities of butter, flour, and provisions, for exportation.

They also possess a number of useful and lucrative manufactures, particularly a very extensive one of earthen ware, which they have brought to great perfection, and supply the whole country with it for some hundred miles around.

In short, although they very carefully preserve themselves from intermixing with, and detached from every other sect, society, or order of people, yet they certainly are valuable subjects, and by their unremitting industry and labour have brought a large extent of wild rugged country into a high state of population and improvement.

It is impossible for me to relate or discover one half of the singular manners, policy, customs, and peculiarities of the Moravians, during the very contracted residence I made amongst them, for I remained there but three days; and what
I have

I have mentioned is only a sketch of their exterior *en passant*.

And as I have no doubt but others have sufficiently explained the principles and minutiæ of the internal government of this sect or fraternity, with the advantages of a better opportunity of information, and superior abilities and knowledge of the subject than I am able to boast of; therefore I conceive it is totally unnecessary for me to enlarge any farther upon that head on this occasion.

Salem, their principal town and settlement, is seven miles from Bethabara, seventeen from Bethania, about forty-five from Salisbury, and near ninety miles from Hillsborough.

It stands on Bellews Creek, a branch of the river Dan, which runs into or rather principally composes the Roanoak; although the other two Moravian towns are built upon branches of the Moravian River, or Creek, which is also pretty considerable, but falls into the Yadkin.

CHAP. XXX.

The Ararat Mountains. Tryon Mountains. Moravian Mountains. Carraway Mountains. Grand and beautiful perspective Views.

IN the ride from Salisbury to Bethania, my sight was frequently regaled with a glimpse of the summit of Tryon mountains on my left, and the stupendous mountain of Ararat directly before me.

Coming from Bethania to Salem, I was extremely pleased with beholding the same mountains of Tryon on my right, the Moravian mountain on my left, and the Carraway Mountains in front, although it was but very seldom I could enjoy that pleasure; *viz.* only in passing over the summits of the high hills, appendages of these mountains.

The Moravian towns and settlements are situated on the base of the south west side of the Moravian Mountains, which are in fact only huge protuberances from,

from, or appendages of, the stupendous Ararat on the north-west, and the Carraway Mountains on the south-east, to which they appear equally to belong.

The soil in general is rich and fertile, the face of the country rocky, broken, and mountainous, though many of the Moravian settlements are choice level spots, and the whole is extremely well watered with excellent streams of that fluid, light, clear, and wholesome, which are likewise converted, by the ingenuity, labour, and industry of the inhabitants, into the useful purposes of turning mills of many different kinds.

On the fourth day after my arrival at Salem I left it, and proceeded on my journey to Hillsborough; and, desiring to see as much of the country as possible, intended to take a very circuitous route to that place, by the lower road over the Allamance, as I had come out by the upper road over the Reedy River on my first journey south-westward.

For

For this purpofe it was neceffary for me to take a long ride along the bafe of the Carraway mountains, between the eaft fide of them and the Deep River, a principal branch of the North-weft or Cape Fear River.

Accordingly, at the diftance of twelve miles from Salem, I arrived at the fummit of the Carraway Mountains, at the north-eaft end of the ridge, an hour after fun-rife.

Here I alighted as ufual, to enjoy the pleafures of the grand, wild, and uncultivated fcene of perfpective around me.

The mountain is nearly half a mile broad on the fummit, and on the fouth-weft brow I firft began to take a retrofpective view of the beautiful fcene which I was now leaving behind me. Tryon Mountain on the weft; the Moravian Mountain on the north, brightened with the beams of the rifing fun, over which the mighty Ararat erected his ftupendous gilded head; the thick embrowned greenifh foreft below, interfected with the multitude of water-courses that fall into the meandering serpentine Yadkin, thinly spotted, as is common in these comprehensive, sylvan perspectives, with the settlements of the inhabitants of the earth, which were now darkened with the vast shadow of the mountains over-hanging them, that had as yet precluded them from a sight of the grand luminary of nature.

Having long gazed with infinite pleasure, and without an alloy of satiety, on these admirable scenes, time, ever advancing, reminded me of the necessity of proceeding, if it was only to behold the equally grand and delightful perspective on the opposite side of the mountain.

This was a more bright and splendid scene than the past, for here the sun gilded every object, and at the same time that the magnitude, wildness, and extent of the view rendered it awful, the serene smiling sky and climate inspired the most pleasing and delightful sensations.

From this situation I could perceive the mountains beyond Haw River, and above
Hills-

Hillsborough, at a vast distance on the left; on the right an extension of view of the ridge of the Carraway Mountains, towering above each other in wild disorder; and in front the sight was bounded by the horizon at an immense distance, verging above the line of which appeared the hills of Allamance, and the high lands on each side of them; and the Deep River below and directly before me winding in beautiful serpentine meanders, as if issuing from underneath the mountain where on I stood, and spreading for a long way under the eye, as if drawn upon a carpet; with the dark chasms containing Reedy River and the numerous other branches of the Haw; but the whole, as is constantly the appearance in this country, an immense unbounded forest, so perfectly overspread and totally covered with thick and seemingly impenetrable woods, that the thinly scattered human settlements can scarcely be ascertained by the eye, lost and confounded in the magnitude, grandeur,

and

and immenſity of the general objects which compoſe the ſurrounding, pleaſing, awful ſcene.

The trees were all juſt putting forth their young and tender foliage, over which the ſun-beams diſplayed a beautiful chearful luſtre. The birds were warbling forth their melodious and variegated notes, welcoming the vegetation of returning ſpring. Odoriferous gales, from every direction, pervaded the whole ſurrounding atmoſphere, with the moſt elegant and grateful perfumes. But ſociety, endearing delightful ſociety, was wanting to form and complete the felicity of man.

CHAP. XXXI.

Great Allamance. Regulators. Hillsborough. Colonel Mac Donald, and the unfortunate Loyalists of North Carolina. Their Disaster at More's Creek Bridge. Their hard Fate and barbarous Treatment.

WITH a solitary sigh, occasioned by, and expressive of, the want of a proper object to share, increase, and to whom I might communicate the pleasures of my imagination and senses, in the enjoyment of this elegant perspective, I left this charming spot (described in the last chapter), and proceeded down the declivity of the mountain.

Having dined at the ordinary at the foot of the Carraway ridge, where I had lodged formerly on my first expedition to the south-westward, at the place where the upper road from Hillsborough to Salisbury crosses this, I arrived at another indifferent house of public entertainment, where I was obliged to take up my residence for the night, after a journey of fifty miles, which, in this rough country, and bad roads, is indeed excessively fatiguing both for the horse and his rider.

Ever since I crossed the mountain I have been descending all day between the Deep River and the base of the Carraway Ridge, and never at any considerable distance from either.

This ordinary, where I lodged, is situated at the crossing of two great public roads, viz. that from the Moravian towns (in which I have journied since I left them), to Wilmington, Brunswick, &c. on the coast of the Atlantic, and the lower road or great trading path from Hillsborough to Salisbury, &c. which now was the way for me to proceed by.

Accordingly, in the morning, I took my left-hand cross-road, and after a long, but pleasant, ride down the eastern side of the Allamance Creek, I arrived at night at the house of a Mr. Michael Holt, a Dutchman, whose plantation was adjoining the creek, near the place where it enters the Haw River; having observed that I rode over a great deal of excel-

excellent land during these two days, the last of which I likewise travelled at least fifty miles.

Mr. Holt, although a High Dutchman, or rather the son of Dutch or German parents, for he himself was born in America, is a very loyal subject, and entertained me with great hospitality. He is a magistrate, possesses a considerable property, and has a large share of good sense and sound judgement, but without the least improvement from education, or the embellishment of any kind of polish, even in his exterior.

In the course of a long interesting conversation, with which he entertained me, and really afforded me a great deal of satisfaction and information by his sensible, blunt, and shrewd remarks on every subject occasionally, he explained the whole grounds, proceedings, and termination of that most unfortunate and much to be lamented affair of the Regulators, which made so great a noise in North Carolina, their scene of action, as well as in all America besides.

But,

But, to avoid throwing reflections and censure, however juft or otherwife, on characters of perfons ftill in exiftence, out of whofe power it is now ever to atone for their former, perhaps ill-timed, unfortunate, and miftaken conduct, I fhall fuffer it to reft in oblivion, only obferving that thofe unhappy, ill-fated victims, the Regulators of North Carolina, were, and ftill are among the worthieft, fteadieft, and moft refpectable friends to Britifh government and real conftitutional freedom. But oppreffion, mifreprefentation, and ill fortune feem ever to have been the attendants on, and inaufpicious fate of exemplary loyalty and virtue.

I left Mr. Holt on the fecond day after breakfaft, and croffing the Haw River, &c. at a very good ford, arrived at Hillfborough to dinner, having rode only about twenty-fix miles.

[This Mr. Holt, of Orange county, fome Americans from Guildford county, almoft all the Chiefs of the former Regulators,

lators, and about fifty or sixty of the principal men of the Scots Highland Emigrants of the settlement of Cross Creek, all under the command of Lieutenant-colonel Donald Mac Donald, as brigadier-general (now in London), having received great encouragement and particular directions from Governor Martin, his Majesty's Governor of North Carolina, to array the loyal inhabitants as militia in arms, who are very numerous in this province, he having promised to support them with arms, ammunition, money, and troops, if they could penetrate as far as Wilmington, or Brunswick, before which he lay at anchor in the river of Cape Fear on board a vessel of war, accordingly raised and arrayed about fifteen hundred men within a few days.

But having very imprudently delayed time for several weeks afterwards, and having committed some other capital blunders and mistakes, which however they were in some measure compelled to do, much againſt Colonel Mac Donald's inclinations, and out of his power to prevent, this afforded the rebels an opportunity to aſſemble and collect in great force from every quarter around, to the number of ſix or eight thouſand men, tolerably well armed, to oppoſe their progreſs.

Yet, in the face of ſo vaſt a ſuperiority, this handful of brave men, without arms for one-ſixth of their number, and even theſe almoſt entirely deſtitute of ammunition, marched boldly on, forcing their way, with great ſpirit and reſolution, for eighty miles to More's Creek Bridge, within ſixteen miles of Wilmington.

Here (on finding themſelves unſupported, Colonel Mac Donald alſo being very ſick, and unable to command) by falling into diviſions and diſſenſions among themſelves and other injudicious meaſures, in attempting to croſs this rivulet in the face of works thrown up and lined by very ſuperior numbers of the enemy under cover, and ſupported likewife by feveral pieces of artillery, at a place where it was not fordable, upon a wooden bridge, the planks of which had been taken up, and the beams and fleepers greafed and rendered flippery and impaffable by the rebels, they met with a total defeat, feveral being killed, (particularly a gallant officer, Captain Mac Leod, &c.) fighting bravely with their broad fwords.

General Mac Donald, who, as I have already mentioned, happened then to be extremely ill, and almoft all their officers being taken prifoners, were treated with the utmoft rigour and barbarity, to a degree fcarcely credible among civilized nations.

Thefe gentlemen were all dragged through the country in triumph, in the moft diftreffed miferable condition, deftitute even of common neceffaries, and were at laft diftributed in prifons and wretched places of reftraint, conftructed for the particular purpofes of cruelty, through the diftant inland parts of Virginia, Maryland, and Penfylvania; and very few of them indeed

deed have ever been able to return to their unhappy, disconsolate, helpless families and homes*.

General Mac Donald, Mr. Holt, and about thirty of the principals persons amongst them, were brought to Philadelphia in that wretched condition, and thrown into prison, where I, being then also in close confinement in the same place, had the melancholy, mortifying satisfaction of seeing and conversing with my old friendly, hospitable Dutchman once more: however, he contrived to make interest with the Congress to permit him to return again to his family and home, which they also granted to all of them who were natives of America, excepting a very worthy officer, Captain Leggit.

But the gallant brave old general, a man then near seventy years of age, who had been almost half a century an officer in his majesty's service, was most ignominiously and inhumanly treated, being rigidly and

* See Chap. xxi. page 169.

cruelly

cruelly confined in a clofe room, fecured with iron doors and bars, along with nine gentlemen befides, in the moft fultry weather, and hot climate, during the fummer; for he magnanimoufly and nobly declined their offers of partial indulgence to himfelf, unlefs it was extended to the reft of his officers, which the Congrefs, to its eternal difgrace and infamy, abfolutely refufed, for no reafon whatfoever but on account of their zealous and exemplary loyalty and refolution.

This worthy old officer General Mac Donald was at length exchanged along with General Prefcott, for an American Colonel Mac Gaw, and the American General Alexander, or pretended Earl of Stirling.

CHAP. XXXII.

Hillsborough. Courts of Judicature. Numbers of Inhabitants in North-Carolina. Depopulation. Bewildered and lost. Uninhabited Forest. Wild Beasts. Great Danger. Hycoe Creek. Country Line Creek.

MY horse, although an excellent one, being, as well as myself, a good deal fatigued and stiff with travelling, I remained three days at Hillsborough, for the benefit of rest and refreshment.

As I observed before, Hillsborough is the capital of a district, of which there are six in the province, where supreme courts of judicature, with extensive and peculiar jurisdictions, are held twice a year: each district contains a certain number of counties, of which there are thirty-two in the whole state. Every county also holds a court quarterly at a court-house erected in the most central place of each; besides those supreme courts for the districts.

Within the whole province of North-Carolina, there is not one good harbour, being

being all obstructed with bars, and fluctuating sand-banks. That of Brunswick and Wilmington on Cape Fear river is the best, but none will admit ships of great burden.

North-Carolina was computed to contain about three hundred thousand inhabitants, in the late calculation made by the Congress, and to have a larger proportion of Whites than any other of the southern provinces, that is, more than a third, and nearly one half. But I am well assured that this calculation was exaggerated above thirty thousand at least; and North-Carolina has decreased in population very much indeed since the commencement of the late fatal hostilities, more in proportion than any other state.

On the fourth day, early in the morning, I set out in great spirits for the lower Sawra towns, on the banks of the Dan river, the largest and most southern branch of the Roanoak, being the first commencement of my journey to Henderson's famed new settlement on Kentucky.

In

In the beginning of this day's ride, I was particularly unfortunate in losing my way among the various, different, perplexing paths and tracks that are met with on the north-west side of Hillsborough, among which no particular road can be distinguished in pre-eminence.

It was also unlucky for me that the greater number of the inhabitants on the plantations, where I called to enquire my way, being Germans, neither understood my questions, nor could render themselves intelligible to me; and the few I chanced to find, that did understand English, being chiefly natives of Ireland, most wretchedly ignorant and uncivilized, could give me no directions to ascertain the right way, having scarcely ever even heard of the name of the Sawras.

By this means I am confident that I rode over the distance of twenty-five miles before I had reached, in a direct line, ten miles from Hillsborough, from whence I had set out in the morning.

At

At length, after infinite difficulty, I discovered something like a path or road, which however could scarcely be ascertained, or followed, having been blazed and marked out some years before, but by its privacy, unfrequented direction, and want of use, had grown up again, so as to be even perceived at all with the utmost trouble.

Its course and continuance however, being pretty straight, enabled me to pursue it, which I did for this whole day with a mind filled and agitated with doubts and dilemmas, without once seeing a house, or the least vestige of a human habitation, from about ten miles north-west of Hillsborough.

The disagreeableness of my situation, and the anxiety of my mind, were not a little aggravated by the uncertainty whether or not this path or road, dull, difficult, and almost indeed imperceptible as it was, actually led towards the Sawra towns; as also, by the total want of food, or any kind of refreshment during the whole day, excepting a draught of water out of a brook running through a

little

little glade or favannah, in which I had alighted, and remained half an hour, for my horfe to feed on the fine luxuriant grafs with which it abounded, who was ſtill lefs able to fubfift without fome kind of nourifhment than I was, on account of the fuperior degree of fatigue he was compelled to undergo.

At the approach of night, my uneafinefs and anxiety increafed to a very heavy and painful degree, for there was no habitation within many miles diftance around me, in the midft of an immenfe, univerfal, gloomy foreft, abounding, and extremely infefted with wild beafts, whofe difmal howls and different horrid yells and cries began to refound through the woods on every fide as night approached; and I was abfolutely deftitute not only of a great-coat, cloak, or blanket, to protect me from the cold of the night, and the dews, but likewife even of the means of making a fire to remain by, which is the only effectual method of preventing the approach of the ravenous wild beafts of the foreft, that might

might otherwife be fo daring as to attack, and perhaps devour the defencelefs traveller.

My apprehenfions were not a little magnified by a total want of confidence in my own abilities as a wood's-man, for in that moft neceffary acquifition, and for travelling in this country, indifpenfible qualification, I was yet a perfect novice, being perpetually fubject to get bewildered and loft in going only the diftance of five miles through the woods without a path.

In my prefent fituation, I had advanced a long day's ride into the heart of this defart and uninhabited foreft, even uncertain whether the almoft imperceptible path I was in, led to the place I wifhed to gain: befides, in the fuppofition that it did lead to it, it muft ftill be at the diftance of another day's ride, which, in every probability, was alfo deftitute of inhabitants, and equally infefted with and abounding in difficulty and dangers.

I had been fo negligent and thoughtlefs as to make little enquiry about this circumftance before I left Hillfborough, and in what

what I did make, could receive no kind of satisfaction, for there was not a single person in or near Hillsborough, who had ever travelled that way.

Nor had I been more provident in laying in some little stock of provision or refreshment, and other conveniences and necessaries for such a journey; never imagining that there were no inhabitants for the greater part of the way.

In this disagreeable, distressing dilemma, and anxious uncertainty, agitated with every painful reflection, I began to think of returning to Hillsborough.

This idea was strong on my mind, during one hour's time, on the approach of night; but still I proceeded on, deliberating on the consequences of the determination either way.

At length, recollecting, that even if I concluded to return, I should be under the necessity of remaining all night in these dismal woods, without a fire, or covering, and destitute of every protection or defence against the approaches and attacks

tacks of the furrounding wild beafts, whofe loud roaring and hideous yells continually affailed mine ears, or elfe I muft travelback again all night: in this cafe I confidered, that as I found fuch difficulty in afcertaining and following this dull path in advancing forwards during this day, with all the advantages of light, it would be abfolutely impoffible to retrace it one hundred yards back in a dark night, the confequences of which muft be, that of being entirely bewildered and loft in the woods, and in all probability, perifhing in the immenfe unbounded foreft, before I could arrive at a human habitation.

Thefe confiderations determined me to perfift in my journey, and to purfue the path forwards to fome fettlement; which, in every human probability, it muft at length conduct me to.

In this refolution I pufhed boldly and brifkly on, until I came to a very confiderable ftream of water, in the low grounds of which I was much puzzled to trace the continuance of the path.

This rivulet is named Hycoe creek (as I have been informed since) and the place where I crossed was so very miry, that my horse had almost sunk down in it under me.

I was now in great expectations of finding some settlement, the land upon each side of this water-course being exceedingly rich and fertile, but, much to my mortification, I travelled through these valuable low grounds, re-ascended the high lands, and rode on some miles, without the least appearance of a human habitation.

At length, to my unspeakable comfort, when hope was almost fled, and the gloom of evening had considerably advanced, I heard the barking of a dog, and the lowing of oxen; I immediately struck out of the path, and endeavoured, by the nearest way through the woods, to gain the place from whence these agreeable and welcome sounds proceeded.

But in this attempt it was my fortune to encounter farther disappointments, and insuperable obstacles, for I soon met with

an

an impenetrable thicket of young hiccory saplings, growing so near to each other, and their branches so perfectly interwoven, and entangled together, that it totally obstructed my farther progress, and compelled me to return to the path I had just left: even this also was a task of difficulty, for in searching after it I was for some time entirely lost and bewildered, before I was able again to discover it.

Having at length found the path, and pursuing it on very eagerly, I soon arrived at the low grounds of another considerable rivulet, which ran in such a serpentine direction, and with so many winding meanders, that the path crossed it five times within the distance of half a mile.

It was now become so dark, and especially in these low grounds, covered and overshadowed with the intermixing branches of the lofty thick woods, of which almost every tree was overgrown with prodigious vines, whose numerous branches and extensive foliage added to the gloom and darkness below, that I could no longer perceive the path, and confequently found it impoffible to proceed much farther.

I was now in a fituation and predicament the moſt difagreeable and diſtreſſing that can be conceived; the ground beneath me wet miry and finking under my horfe, his legs entangled in the vines, bambooes, briars, bruſh and under-wood, which prevented him from proceeding in any direction; the path entirely loft, not knowing even on which fide I had deviated from it; infects, reptiles, and ferpents of the moſt poifonous, deadly, and fatal nature, fwarming in the woods, and on the ground, and the wild beaſts howling hideouſly around me; the night exceſſively dark, overcaſt and threatening rain; no poſſibility of ftriking a light, or making a fire, and totally unprotected and defencelefs againſt the attacks of all thofe furrounding, formidable foes.

CHAP.

CHAP. XXXIII.

Mr. Hart. A moſt hoſpitable, benevolent Perſon. An accompliſhed Gentleman. Agreeable Surpriſe. Fortunate Eſcape. Mr. Bayly. Strange Manner of Lodging. A lovely Girl. Sawra Towns. Sawra Nation. Upper Sawra Towns.

MY ſituation, as repreſented in the concluſion of the laſt chapter, was not rendered leſs mortifying by the certainty of a houſe and inhabitants being near, which was put beyond a doubt by the lowing of the oxen and the barking of the dogs, that I had heard, although I had found it impracticable to reach the place from whence thoſe deſirable ſounds ſeemed to proceed.

At length I bethought myſelf of calling out as loud as I was able. This expedient ſucceeded to my wiſh, for, after I had hallooed ſeveral times as loudly as I could vociferate, to my great ſurprize and inexpreſſible ſatisfaction and pleaſure, I was anſwered by a human voice, which ſeemed to come from ſome perſon on an eminence, juſt above the ſpot whereon I was fixed.

However, being unable to approach the place where he was, I continued to call aloud, and was regularly anfwered by the fame voice, until in a fhort time a Negro arrived at the difmal thicket wherein I was faft entangled.

It was with the utmoft difficulty, and a confiderable time before he was able to extricate me from this perplexing and perilous fituation, but at length he effected it, and brought me once more to the comfortable and much-wanted affiftance of fociety.

The poor Negro himfelf, although accuftomed to the woods, appeared aftonifhed at the dangerous and dreadful fituation in which he found me, and feemed almoft equally rejoiced with myfelf at my fortunate deliverance.

The houfe and plantation to which the Negro flave conducted me, belonged to a Mr. Hart his mafter, who received and entertained me with the greateft hofpitality and kindnefs; but what added to my aftonifhment and agreeable furprize was, to find the proprietor, not only a polished member of society, but almost an accomplished and complete gentleman.

To meet with such a person in the wild back woods of America, in a situation the most recluse, solitary and unfrequented, and at so great a distance from the inhabitants, who are themselves little better, perhaps much worse, than savages, especially at a time when I stood so much in need of assistance, was altogether unexpected, and afforded me a gratification and pleasure, thus enhanced by these attending circumstances, not to be described in language.

The refreshments, comforts, and consolation he bestowed upon me with a liberal hand, appeared to afford even a superior degree of satisfaction and felicity to him, than to me; and he pressed me to remain there the day following, which was wet and rainy, to rest and refresh both myself and my horse, and to recover from the severe fatigue and hardships we had undergone.

In the courfe of the enfuing day, we took an opportunity of vifiting. and more narrowly examining the fpot wherein I had been ftopt, and from whence the Negro had extricated me. The flave conducted us to it.

It was indeed the moft difagreeable and dangerous place imaginable: a deep miry fwamp overgrown with briars, bambooes, and poifonous vines, among which my horfe and I had been fo perplexed and entangled.

Fortunate it was for us both that we met with thofe impediments, for had we proceeded only ten yards farther, both my horfe and myfelf muft have inevitably perifhed in a quagmire, or deep morafs, from which no poffible affiftance could have refcued or preferved us.

We returned to the houfe, admiring with gratitude at this hair-breadth providential deliverance, and early on the morning following I took my laft farewell of the humane benevolent Mr. Hart, and proceeded on my journey, very little better provided againft contingencies than before,

before, but perfectly refreshed and recovered from my fatigue, with my horse also in high spirits.

The last mentioned rivulet, the low grounds of which had been the scene of my principal difficulties and perils, and on the high land adjoining it the worthy and benevolent Mr. Hart's plantation was situated, is named Country Line creek.

There is a small settlement on the choice land on the banks of these two rivulets, the Hycoe and the Country Line, which are confiderable streams of water, that run into the Dan River at the distance of fifty miles from this place.

Having made a very early breakfast before I departed, and having been shown the continuance of the former dull, difficult, blind path, whose direction to the Sawra Towns was now ascertained to my sufficient satisfaction, I travelled during all this long day likewise, until late in the afternoon, without once discovering the least vestige of a human settlement, or habitation.

But

But about that time, as I advanced on the fummit of a confiderable hill, I could plainly perceive mountains, vaft valleys, and deep chafms, precipices, and ravines on my right: for I obferved, that the face of the country had been becoming more and more uneven, broken, and rugged, and the eminences had been gradually fwelling into higher hills, as I proceeded on, for the laft ten or twelve miles.

I now perceived a path on my right, which appeared plainer than that I had travelled in fo long: this raifed my doubts, but at length determined me to continue to purfue that which was the dulleft.

Fortunately for me, my decifion was right in this inftance, for in the evening I arrived at the Sawra Towns, after encountering fome further difficulties in afcertaining the right way among the variety of different tracks I met with immediately on entering the vicinity of the fettlement.

At the Sawra Towns, I lodged at the houfe of a Mr. Bailey, on the banks of the

river

river Dan, a common plain back wood's planter, with a large family of Bel Savages, a hofpitable, but uncultivated mind, and rude manners.

Mr. Bailey had only one room, and one bed, in his houfe, on which he and his wife were accuftomed to fleep: this they very kindly offered to accommodate me with, but as they were advanced in years, and I was young and healthy, although fuperior in rank and appearance to them, I could not think of accepting their very generous offer, but took my chance on a pallet fpread on the floor from one fide of the room to the other, on which every perfon of the family, excepting the mafter and miftrefs, lay promifcuoufly, men and women, boys and girls.

The weather being uncommonly warm, I found the pallet by far the moft agreeble place of repofe, and I arofe early in the morning with the reft of the family, which confifted, befides fome flaves and his fmall children the little boys and girls, of feveral fons grown up to maturity, and
three

three young women his daughters, the youngeſt of whom was juſt fifteen years old, a moſt lovely charming brunette, named Betſy, of a ſhape and features perfectly exquiſite and expreſſive, and endued with a mind and manners, mild, gentle, and delicate, yet quite in a ſtate of nature, unincumbered with poliſhed refinements or faſhionable ceremony, and unimproved by education, acquired knowledge, and modern accompliſhments,

Mr. Bailey and all his family joined in entreating me to ſtay with them ſome days; and, as I really ſtood in great need of reſt and refreſhment, it was with infinite ſatisfaction that I complied with their very friendly hoſpitable requeſt.

During ten days that I remained at the Sawra Towns, I found the lovely Betſy my kind friend and conſtant companion. She endeavoured to pleaſe, and ſhe gave delight. Although truly, and in the moſt liberal ſenſe, the child of nature, without an alloy either of art or diſſimulation, I actually diſcovered in her mind a degree
of

of generofity, fentiment, and the moft delicate fenfibility, that very few of the more polifhed and accomplifhed ladies can boaft of.

She abfolutely gained on my affections every moment, and it required the utmoft exertions of refolution to tear myfelf at laft from her delightful company. But the image of the lovely Betfy Bailey can never be erafed from my mind, and it is with pleafure I cherifh her remembrance.

The Sawras, although once a confiderable nation of Indians, have been long extinct: there is not even a fingle family or trace of them remaining, excepting thefe veftiges of their towns, which ftill continue to fupport their name, this being fortunately preferved as the appellation of thefe two fettlements.

The upper Sawra Towns are trifling and infignificant, compared with the lower Sawra Towns, which is an extremely valuable fettlement: and although I found more fatigue, and greater hardfhips, difficulties, and dangers in my journey hither, than in all my former travels through America,

America, this place is not more than sixty-five miles from Hillsborough, and ninety-five from Salisbury, in the same county with the latter, viz. that of Roan, it is situated; being within only a very few miles of the northern boundary line of the province of North-Carolina.

CHAP.

CHAP. XXXIV.

Dan River. Strange and singular Phenomenon. Great Extent. Lower Sawra Towns. A vast and profitable Purchase. Horn, or Hoop Snake. Most poisonous. Alarming Accounts of the Indians.

THE river Dan, at the lower Sawra towns, is near six hundred yards wide, rocky, rapid, bold, and containing a vast body of water; it arises in the Alegany mountains, near to the source of the river Ararat, a branch of the Yadkin, and at no great distance from the New River, which is the upper part, or most southward branch of the Great Kanhaway that falls into the Ohio.

The Dan is the largest of three great rivers, namely, the Dan, the Bannister, and the Stanton, which at their confluence compose the Roanoak, and in all appearance this river alone, at the Sawra towns, contains a greater quantity of water than the Roanoak itself at Halifax, which is above two hundred miles below, and then it has received near an hundred large

large rivulets, besides the other two great rivers, the Bannister and the Stanton, in its course between these two places; yet the Dan, at the Sawra towns, is nearly twice as wide as the Roanoak is at Halifax.

This is a phenomenon difficult to be accounted for, and only reconciled to my ideas, or understanding, by the supposition of the vast quantity of water evaporated by the intensely hot beams of the sun, and by the air, during its course, and by still a more enormous proportion being constantly absorbed in the sandy soil through which it passes during the latter part of its progress.

I must confess that this solution is by no means a sufficient eclaircissement, therefore I shall not hazard any farther explanation, or conjecture, but leave it to the exercise of more ingenious minds, contenting myself with the bare relation of the mere matter of fact.

The length of this river from the source of the Dan, in the Alegany mountains,

tains, to Roanoak inlet on the coaft of the Atlantic Ocean, is very extenfive, being more than fix hundred miles along with the meanders, and not lefs than five hundred miles in a direct line.

'The whole fettlement of the lower Sawra Towns, being a vaft body of excellent and moft valuable land, containing thirty-three thoufand acres, of which more than nine thoufand are exceedingly rich low grounds, is the property of Mr. Farley, of the ifland of Antigua in the Weft Indies, and formerly belonged to the late Col. William Byrd, of Weftover, on James River, in Virginia.

'About the year feventeen hundred and fixty-one, Mr. Byrd fold the whole of this large, valuable, and extenfive tract of land to a Mr. Maxwell, for only five hundred pounds, who concluded the purchafe without feeing it.'

'In the fpring of the enfuing year, he went out to view his new eftate.'

'It happened, juft at that time, that a prodigious flood in the Dan had overfpread the whole of the low lands on the river, of which near ten thousand acres were covered by the inundation.

This extraordinary circumstance, and very awful appearance, astonished and intimidated Mr. Maxwell, who, on his return to Westover, expressing dissatisfaction with his purchase, Mr. Byrd, with a generosity for which he was distinguished, returned him the five hundred pounds, and received again the property of his lands.

That same year, in the fall, or autumn, Mr. Farley of Antigua, being on a visit at Westover, in Virginia, and having understood that Col. Byrd had a large tract of excellent land in the back country to dispose of, after being informed of the number of acres, immediately offered one thousand pounds for the purchase, without ever having seen it also; which offer was as readily accepted.

Mr. Farley, having returned to Antigua, suffered it to remain in this uncultivated, unimproved state, and never went near it, until the year one thousand seven hundred and sixty-nine, when he sent his son, James Parke

Parke Farley, Esq. into Virginia, who ventured out that distance into the back country to view the estate, and after some difficulty in removing accidental settlers, who had taken possession of such parts thereof as they best approved without any legal right or authority, divided it into numerous plantations and farms, which he rented out, keeping in his own hands, a most valuable excellent tract, the choice of the whole; on this plantation he settled a great number of slaves, and a vast stock, all of which also increased prodigiously.

In short the value of this estate has augmented so exceedingly, that in the year seventeen hundred and seventy-two, Mr. Farley refused twenty-eight thousand pounds for the purchase of it. A mortifying circumstance and reflection this to Mr. Byrd, the first proprietor, who had transacted the business, and was then in existence and necessity; but somewhat alleviated by the younger Mr. Farley, in whose possession it was, having inter-married with his eldeſt daughter, ſo that by this means the eſtate was not entirely out of the family.

During the ten days of my reſidence at this place, we had frequent alarming accounts of the attacks, depredations, and ſhocking barbarities committed by the Indians on the White inhabitants, ſome diſtance beyond the Dan, about the head of Smith's River which falls into the Dan on the north ſide, almoſt oppoſite to the lower Sawra Towns.

This induced Mr. Bailey and his family, particularly the lovely, amiable Betſy, to be very ſtrenuous and preſſing in perſuading me to defer the proſecution of my intended journey, and to proceed no farther, on account of the hardſhips, difficulties, and imminent dangers I muſt inevitably encounter, at this inauſpicious period, in the purſuit of this propoſed expedition to Henderſon's new ſettlement on Kentucky, which was ſtill a prodigious diſtance from me, no leſs than five hundred miles, and through the Indian country the greater part of the way.

They

They all very urgently and kindly requested me to remain along with them during the enſuing ſummer; and had I at that time attended and given way to the bias of my inclinations, and the feelings of my heart, I ſhould certainly have embraced their hoſpitable propoſal with infinite pleaſure.

But when I maturely conſidered the fatal conſequences of yielding to the pleaſing allurements of the ſenſes, and the uncontrouled ſway of the paſſions, at my early period of life, I ſummoned up all my fortitude and reſolution to ſupport and aſſiſt me in the conflict, determined to perſiſt in my original undertaking, however perilous, and tear myſelf from this enchanting, but dangerous ſtate of felicity,

I therefore finally concluded to proceed, notwithſtanding the hazard and jeopardy attending my farther progreſs, ariſing from the alarming commotions of the Indians, which were now indeed ſufficiently aſcertained and authenticated.

When I related to Mr. Bailey the difficulty and hardſhips I had already encountered in my journey out to the Sawra Towns, he informed me, that the road or path, along which I had travelled, was firſt made and blazed about nine years before; but that it had been ſo very little frequented, and the buſhes and underwood had grown up again ſo perfectly, that when he had occaſion to go to Hillſborough, about two years ago, he could ſcarcely perceive it at all; but having a tomahawk with him, he blazed the trees on each ſide, as he went along, by which means he was enabled the more readily to find his way in returning; and that it was the remaining appearance of his blazing on the trees, by which I had been able to trace the path, elſe it muſt have been totally impracticable for me to have found or followed it at all; for he believed no perſon whatever, excepting himſelf and me, had travelled it for ſeveral years paſt, and very few indeed had ever uſed it, ſince its firſt exiſtence.

The

The reason of its being so much unfrequented was, because what little intercourse and trade the inhabitants of the Sawra settlements carried on with the sea-ports, and more cultivated part of the country, was either by roads down along the side of the Dan and the Roanoak to Halifax, and Edenton, in North-Carolina, or across the country to Petersburg, and Richmond, &c. on James River, in Virginia.

While I was at the Sawra Towns, one day a little lad of Mr. Bayley's came to acquaint us that he had killed a horn snake, which being a curiosity that I was extremely desirous of observing and examining with particular attention, I accompanied him to the place where he said he had left it; but when we arrived there, to my great disappointment it was not to be found.

He assured me that it must not have been quite dead, and had recovered so much as to be able to crawl from the spot on which he had left it, and had secreted itself somewhere among the leaves.

However, every one, and all the inhabitants, with the greatest confidence asserted and avowed their having seen such snakes, though very seldom.

They represented them to me, as the most formidable and direful foes in existence to the human race, and to all animation; poisonous and fatal to a degree almost beyond credibility.

'He is described as something resembling a black snake, but thicker, shorter, and of a colour more inclining to a dark brown. He never bites his adversary, but has a weapon in his tail, called his sting, of a hard, horny substance, in shape and appearance very much like to a cock's spur: with this he strikes his antagonist, or whatever object he aims at, when he least expects it, and if it penetrates the skin, it is inevitable and sudden death.

So very virulent is his poison, that it is reported, if he should miss the object he pointed at, and should strike his horn through the bark of a young sapling tree, if it penetrates into the sap or vital juice, the bark or rind will, within a few hours, swell, burst, and peel off, and the tree itself will perish.

As other serpents crawl upon their bellies, so can this; but he has another method of moving peculiar to his own species, which he always adopts when he is in eager pursuit of his prey; he throws himself into a circle, running rapidly round, advancing like a hoop, with his tail arising and pointing forward in the circle, by which he is always in the ready position of striking.

It is observed, they only make use of this method in attacking; for when they fly from their enemy, they go upon their bellies, like other serpents.

From the above circumstance, peculiar to themselves, they have also derived the appellation of hoop snakes.

Being firmly resolved to proceed on my expedition to Kentucky, I endeavoured to hire a guide from this place, but every one that I applied to declined it, both because they were as little acquainted with the way as myself, and on account of the
dif-

disturbances, and violent outrages lately committed by the Indians, at which every person without exception was terrified in the highest degree.

They also endeavoured to communicate their panic, fears, and apprehensions to me; but my ignorance of the actual danger enabled me to resist, with effect, every attack of that nature, and determined me, although I could not obtain either a servant, guide, or companion, to persist in the enterprize, however hazardous; and I even concluded to set out alone.

CHAP.

CHAP. XXXV.

Ford the Dan. Fall in. Part with my lovely Guide. Get loſt. Perplexing Situation. Come upon a Number of Indians. Their Behaviour. Their Hoſpitality and Kindneſs.

ON the fifteenth day of May I took my leave of Mr. Bailey and his family, every one of whom ſeemed to be really more concerned for my future ſafety than I could poſſibly have conceived, being all in tears, and appearing almoſt certain that I ſhould be deſtroyed by the ſavages; having uſed their moſt earneſt perſuaſions and utmoſt endeavours to change my reſolution of proceeding on this journey.

The kind-hearted and truly amiable Betſy inſiſted on piloting me over the Dan herſelf, rather than any of her brothers, although the ford at this place was extremely rapid, rocky, and dangerous, particularly to thoſe unacquainted therewith and with the intricate manner of paſſing it, the river being alſo very wide.

This

This I experienced to my coſt, for being rather inattentive in following quite cloſe to my beautiful young Amazonian conductor, who was on horſeback, riding boldly like a man, my horſe ſuddenly plunged with me into a deep place over both our heads, and we were carried down the current, a conſiderable diſtance, with great velocity.

Indeed it was with the utmoſt difficulty I reached the oppoſite ſhore at all, after the greateſt hazard imaginable of being loſt, notwithſtanding both my horſe and myſelf were excellent ſwimmers.

The concern of my lovely guide during this dangerous ſcene was inexpreſſible, and only equalled by her joy on my ſafe arrival on ſhore; the banks of which being ſo ſoft, ſteep, and interwoven with roots of trees, which entangled my horſe's legs ſo much, that I could ſcarcely get him up at all: however, at length I accompliſhed it after ſeveral violent ſtruggles.

There being no inhabitants on this ſide of the river, they having all abandoned their plantations, and fled into a
ſtockaded

stockaded fort, about thirty miles distance from thence, where they had taken refuge, upon some of them being found killed by the Indians, I was obliged to strike a light, and kindle a fire in the woods to dry my cloaths; in this my kind companion was as usual very serviceable to me, and in a little more than an hour we set out again on the journey, she insisting to accompany me some miles farther, in order to conduct me the right way which she represented as particularly intricate and difficult to find during that distance.

When we had rode about seven miles together, perceiving my lovely guide make no offer of returning, I insisted on our parting, on account of the extreme danger every person appeared to apprehend from the Indians by their having all left their habitations, which we found deserted and empty for the whole way on that side of the Dan.

Having at length, by an effort of all my resolution, overcome the struggle of parting with this lovely, kind, and affectionate friend, I was seized with a
kind

kind of languor, or carelessness of my fate, my mind and spirits being enervated and softened down with an inexpressibly painful sensibility, which rendered me regardless of whatever might befal me, and indeed quite inattentive to my way, so that in a very few hours, by pursuing the wrong path, I found myself in the woods without any tract whatever to direct my course, that in which I had been having terminated, being only made by the hogs, which run wild almost all over America, and especially in the western frontiers.

It was this disagreeable situation that first roused me from this lethargic, but painful reverie in which I had been absorbed, and I then eagerly pushed on in hopes, yet very doubtful, of finding some path to direct me, and indeed to enable me to travel at all, for it is with great difficulty a person on horseback can pass on through the woods at all where there is no path, on account of the roughness of the ground, the thickets of underwood, the

branches

branches of trees hanging low and intermingling with each other, and the numerous water-courses which are frequently altogether impassable for many miles.

It is impossible for me to ascertain how far I had travelled in this most disagreeable of all imaginable situations, when all on a sudden, on the side of a gentle ascent, I perceived a number of men sitting on the ground, and such they were as I had never seen before, painted black and red, and all armed with firelocks and tomahawks.

I was within the distance of fifty yards of them before I perceived them, [and was absolutely rejoiced to fall in with them, my first idea being that they were hunters, white men, who frequently continue in the woods hunting, for several months together, without going near the inhabitants, or entering a house.

In this idea I immediately went up towards them with joy in my countenance, for in my bewildered condition it was really a pleasure to me to see any of my fellow-crea-

creatures once more, and I did not know nor conceive danger, even from Indians.

But the inftant they perceived me, one of them fell proftrate on the ground, and another jumped on his feet, put his hands to his mouth, and fent forth a moft dreadful yell that made the whole woods refound; and feeing me coming boldly up towards them, he advanced a few fteps to meet me, fpoke fome words I did not underftand, and after paufing a while, held forth his hand towards me: I fhook him heartily by the hand, and faid *I was very glad to meet with them, for I was loft; and intreated they would be fo kind as direct me the way to Beaver Creek and Smith's River.*

He answered again in a language that was to me altogether unintelligible, and I then found they were Indians; which difcovery, however, did not at all alarm or intimidate me, becaufe of my ignorance of the danger I was in.

Obferving one of them point to a broad gold lace and ftone buckle which was

round

round the crown of my hat and glittered in the sun, I alighted from my horse, took it off, and buckled it round the head of him who had shaken hands with me and appeared to be the chief person among them. He seemed much pleased with the present, and made signs for me to sit down and eat with them: this I readily complied with, and partook of a repast, which consisted of venison, kernels of hickory nuts, and wall-nuts, all mixed together with wild honey, and every one eat with his hands, dipping one of them into the victuals.

'To be sure there was neither delicacy nor cleanliness in their manner of eating together, but the food was delicious, and exquisitely pleasant to the taste; and for my own part, having a keen appetite, I eat very heartily, which seemed to afford a particular satisfaction to my hospitable savage friends, for such indeed they were to me.

CHAP. XXXVI.

Directed the Way by the Indians. Leatherwood Creek. Plantations abandoned. Beaver Creek. Arrive at the Fort. Refused Admittance.

MY horse, who had quite as much need of refreshment as me, was also regaling himself on the herbage, for I had turned him loose when I sat down to this Indian primitive feast.

The Indians and I made a shift to keep up a kind of conversation by signs and gestures, for I did not understand a single word of their language, and I did not then imagine that they understood me; but since that time I have had many reasons to believe that English was not altogther unintelligible to some of them, although they either could not, or would not attempt to speak it.

For after both I and my horse were sufficiently refreshed, having staid with them all night, one of the Indians was dif-

dispatched along with me, by him to whom I had made the prefent, and accompanied me for feven or eight miles, to put me into the right way to Beaver Creek, upon Smith's River; and after he had done fo, and pointed out the courfe for me to proceed in, we fhook hands and parted, he returned to his companions, and I purfued my journey along a very plain blazed path, that foon brought me to a large water-courfe, named Leatherwood Creek, which empties itfelf into Smith's River, a very capital branch of the Dan, the confluence of which is about four miles above the lower Sawra Towns, on the north fide.

There were feveral fine plantations on the rich low grounds of this creek, but they were all deferted, not a fingle inhabitant was to be feen; their cattle, horfes, &c. were wandering about their mafter's habitations, and conveyed to me the moft mournful, melancholy, and difmal ideas that can be conceived.

About eight miles beyond Leatherwood Creek, I met a man on horfeback, whofe horfe was covered with foam and fweat.

He feemed to be in the utmoft aftonifhment at the fight of me, and afked me, " Where, in the name of God, I came " from?" I anfwered him, I came yefterday from the Sawra Towns, and was on my way to the fort on Smith's River.

He then exclaimed, " Good God! did " not I know that the Indians had taken " up the hatchet, and had begun to kill " the Whites?" and looking on the ground, " declared he faw their tracts," or the marks of their footfteps " there then;" and afked me " if I had not feen any of " them? But why (faid he) do I afk " you that? If you had feen them, or " they had feen you, I certainly fhould " not have met you here, for they would " either have fcalped you, or have put " you to death by their tortures."

I replied, " he was miftaken, for I had " feen them, had ate and flept with them,

and

" and that they had been very kind to me,
" inſtead of ſcalping me, or putting me to
" death, as he imagined:" but he waited
not to hear the laſt words of what I ſaid,
for as ſoon as he underſtood that I had ſeen
them, he clapped whip and ſpurs to his
horſe back again, as faſt as he could make
him go, while I gazed after him, imagining
the man was mad or delirious.

I rode on at my leiſure, wondering at
this man's ſtrange conduct, and compar-
ing it with that of the Indians towards
me, it was not at all to their diſadvan-
tage.

I ſoon afterwards croſſed another large
water-courſe named Beaver Creek, not
far from the fort, which alſo empties itſelf into Smith's River.

Upon this ſtream there was a very
fine corn or griſt mill, which was alſo
abandoned by the proprietor, and had
been left ſo ſuddenly, that the hopper
remained half full of corn unground,
while the other half was ground into
meal, and in this condition it continued,

the water being turned off from the mill-wheel.

Here I alighted, and fed my horse, and after he had eaten until he left, set out again on my journey.

In riding about two or three miles farther, I at length came to the fort itself, which contained all the inhabitants of the country around, men, women, and children crouded all together.

I was exceedingly happy at the thoughts of being once more among inhabitants, but this imaginary felicity was of very short duration, for when I went to the gate of the fort, expecting to go in, I was positively refused admittance.

My astonishment at this strange unaccountable conduct towards me could only be equalled by my concern at so grievous a disappointment and mortification, for all my entreaties and most earnest solicitations for permission to enter were in vain.

They within insisted that I was an enemy, or a Frenchman, because I had been in company with the Indians, and had

had escaped unmolested, and also as my accent was different from theirs.

This I found they were informed of by the man whom I met on horseback, and who turned back full speed as soon as I acquainted him of my having been with the Indians.

This man, it seems, had been dispatched as an express to the next fort, which was a considerable distance off, for assistance; and had also been directed to reconnoitre the country between; to discover, if he could, what danger was to be apprehended; whether the Indians were doing mischief; and what numbers of them were in the vicinity.

How well he executed his commission, his conduct, already related, evinces; as also how totally unfit he was for such a purpose, having fled with the utmost precipitation on even hearing of Indians, without waiting to discover whether they were hostile or friendly.

CHAP.

CHAP. XXXVII.

Threaten to set Fire to the Fort. Admitted. Shocking Scenes of Iniquity and Obsceneness within. Ride o t and visit the Plantations around. Resolve to set out on my Journey.

I Continued to entreat for admittance until they threatened to fire upon me if I did not retire, which made me withdraw from the gate to consider what steps I must pursue, for I never found myself in so singular and unpleasant a predicament in my life.

However, the first thing I did was to turn my horse loose into a very fine field of green wheat that I observed on the banks of the river; and I wandered all round the country adjacent to the fort for several hours, totally at a loss what to do, or in what manner to proceed.

This was what is called a stockaded fort, but to any person, excepting those who have seen such in America, it would appear

pear in no refpect a place of arms, for there is nothing like an efplanade, counterfcarp, nor ditch, neither ramparts nor parapet, no out-poft, out-centry, nor videttes; but it refembled a quadrangular polygon, inclofed with large timber, and cuts of treesfplit in two, about twelve or fixteen feet high above the ground, ftanding erect, and about three or four feet in the earth, and quite clofe together, with loop holes cut through about four or five feet from the ground for fmall arms.

There was alfo fomething like a baftion at each angle, which, however, could fcarcely be faid to flank the curtains; and a log-houfe, mufket proof, on each fide of the gate.

Within the area, nearly in the centre, was a common houfe framed and boarded, filled in, to the height of fix feet, with ftones and clay on the infide, as a defence againft fmall arms; it was covered only with fhingles made of pine, which could be eafily fet on fire as well as

every

every other part of the whole ſtructure, without exception.

I wandered round and round this fortreſs until night began to advance, and then ventured to approach the gate once more, ſoliciting for admittance, but with no better ſucceſs than before.

I uſed every argument my mind could ſuggeſt to induce them to receive me; put them in mind I was but one man, and deſired them to put me under guard if they ſuſpected me after I was in, if they would only admit me; and beginning alſo to be under apprehenſions for my own life, as the Indians would certainly be tempted to kill a perſon they ſaw ſtraggling round the outſide of the fort, although they did not moleſt me when I came up to them at a diſtance from it; and I alſo conſidered that although one party of them ſpared my life, another party might make no ſcruple of killing me, eſpecially in ſo unfavourable a ſituation; this certain danger inſpired me with a deſperate determination,

tion, and I resolutely told them at the gate, that I must come in, represented the fatal consequences of my being left outside, and positively declared that I would absolutely set fire to the fort if they persisted in refusing me admittance.

They again threatening to shoot me, I assured them that I would as soon be killed by them as by the Indians, and solemnly swore I would set fire to the stockades.

Upon this, I was desired to wait a few minutes, until they consulted together; at the conclusion of which they agreed to admit me.

The wicker gate was then opened, and I crept in; but, good God! such a sight as was presented before mine eyes can scarcely be conceived in idea, much less described.

Such a motley crew of men, women, and children; such an abandoned set of miscreants, void of shame, but abounding with fear; such horrid imprecations, blasphemy, obscenenefs, and every species
of

of iniquity, I never before nor since have seen or heard of.

No subordination, no regularity, no propriety, no good conduct, not a single good word, I had almost said good thought, was there within those gates; but all was confusion, nastiness, and the most abominable wickedness.

To describe the detestable scenes of depravity that I was hourly witness of in this place, would be extremely irksome to myself, and disgusting to others; and on this account I shall pass them all over, only observing, that a set of more wicked, abandoned, shameless, and profligate miscreants never were nor can be collected together.

On the next day I proposed to take a walk about the fort, but they would not let me out at the gate.

However, on the day following I insisted upon it, and they threatened not to admit me again: but notwithstanding, I ventured out, and having saddled my horse, rode a great many miles round the country,

country, without seeing a single inhabitant, or Indian.

I returned to the fort at night, and was admitted; having acquainted them with my obfervations, and the diftance I had reconnoitred around, two young men propofed to accompany me next day, to vifit their father's plantations.

Accordingly we three fet out from the fort early in the morning, and went to one of their plantations, which was five miles off, where we found every thing unmolefted, only the domeftic animals were almoft ftarved, and appeared rejoiced to fee us.

The other plantation was twelve miles diftant from this, and we vifited it alfo; here a tame bear, which had been left, diverted us very much with his antic geftures, and his odd manner of faluting his two-legged brothers whom I had brought with me from the fort: but as, fooner or later, all, even the deareft of friends, muft part, fo muft they, and the forrow on the occasion was great, even as their joy had been, when they met.

We visited several other plantations, and the two young men concluding to return next day to their plantations to remain, we turned our horses heads towards the fort, where we arrived in the evening.

Having made our report concerning the occurrences of the day, and the appearance of peace and tranquility we had every where perceived, it was proposed for each person to return to his respective habitation on the day following; but timidity, distrust, and cowardice started a number of objections, which occasioned many warm debates on the subject; and at length it was concluded on to wait a few days longer, but in the mean time to dispatch two men on each quarter, to see that all was quiet, and that there was no appearance of Indians.

For my own part I determined on setting out early next morning to pursue my journey

ney to Kentucky, having hired one of the young men, who accompanied me in our ride round the fort, to attend me in this journey, which he undertook to do with great alacrity, and seemed as eager to see that celebrated place as myself.

CHAP.

CHAP. XXXVIII.

Situation of the Fort. Smith's River. Soil. Ginseng, Snake-root. Prices of Wheat, Corn, Beef, Pork, Tobacco, &c. Culture of Indian Corn. Its great and universal Utility.

THIS fort is situated on a small eminence that commands a very fine view of Smith's River for several miles, and of the confluence of Beaver Creek; but it is only the low grounds of the river and creek on the north-east side that can be perceived; the lofty timber on the opposite banks of the river, as usual all over America, effectually prevents any greater distance being seen.

But the eminence, the fort is built upon, is by no means the highest in the vicinity; there are many, and some of them almost close to it, that altogether command it.

The low land on Smith's River and Beaver Creek is indeed excellent, but narrow: the high ground and hills, being very near the river on each side, are exceedingly

ceedingly rocky and fteril; the roads, or rather paths, are as bad as can be conceived; and the houfes and plantations are very indifferent indeed; but there is a great abundance of game, fuch as deer, bears, fome panthers, wild cats, otters, raccoons, oppoffums, wild turkeys, and all kinds of fquirrels.

The growth of the timber on the low land is very large, but not equal to that on the low grounds of the Roanoak and the Dan: the foil is of a deep black colour, and rather light, but exceeding deep; however it is liable to be flooded.

The river is about fifty yards wide, but very much interrupted with old logs, large trees, &c. that have been brought down the ftream by the floods after heavy rains; it is not rapid, but flows calmly along, in a fmooth, gentle current, and it is fordable but in a very few places.

The high land, as I obferved before, is very rough, rocky, and poor; fome of it is rather light, and there is abundance of the valuable plant, or rather root of Ginseng found and gathered in the woods, which in China is accounted a specific for almost every disorder incident to the human frame, and sells for more than its weight in gold; here it sells for about fifteen pence currency, or a shilling sterling a pound.

The inhabitants, and negroes, likewise find and dig great quantities of snake-root, of each of the different kinds, which they also sell for nearly the same price as ginseng: this was exported to Europe, being sent by land-carriage to James River, where it was shipped, and British manufactures were taken in exchange for this as well as the rest of all their commodities, at very advanced prices.

They also sell great numbers of deer skins and furs; but the principal of their exports are hogs, which they raise in great numbers, and drive them, in droves of one, two, three, four, and five hundred together, to the falls of James River, and of Roanoak, and to the more populous parts of the country, as well as the sea-ports.

Some few black cattle are also brought from this part of the frontiers, but in no considerable numbers.

Deer skins, dried or cured with the hair on, are sold for about a shilling sterling a pound. Raccoon skins, about six-pence each. Otter skins, about two or three shillings each. Beaver, &c. in proportion.

Their hogs they sell alive, for about twelve shillings an hundred weight, that is, if they are bought there; but when driven down the country, they cost about twenty shillings sterling a hundred weight.

Black cattle sell nearly for the same prices.

Venison is excessively cheap, generally about half-a-crown for a whole deer, exclusive of the skin.

There is also a considerable quantity of tobacco cultivated here, which is almost all carried to James River, and sells there at the rate generally of sixteen, eighteen, or twenty shillings per hundred weight.

They make very little wheat, and use still less; the general price of wheat there at
home

home is about half-a-crown per bushel, which is the measure they sell it by.

But the great support of the country is Indian corn, with which they subsist themselves, their negroes, their horses, and fatten their hogs, after they are in good plight by feeding on the acorns in the woods, which are always called *Mast* in America; of this there are some years amazing quantities, so that the hogs are frequently fattened with that alone, which they find themselves in the woods; but the pork is always soft, and for that reason, people generally feed them some little time upon Indian corn, after they appear sufficiently fatted with mast.

Indian corn is the great staff of life in America, and is measured by what is called the barrel there, which contains just five bushels, and the price then was a dollar, or four shillings and six pence sterling per barrel.

This however was accounted dear, for the general price is only three shillings per barrel, which is not quite seven pence halfpenny

halfpenny a bushel: the cheapest grain perhaps in the world; for it weighs from fifty to fifty-five pounds each the bushel.

As the culture of Indian corn is unknown in Great Britain, or at any rate but very little practised, a brief description of it may not be unacceptable.

Indian corn, which is in some places called Maize, is nearly as large as horse beans, being somewhat flat and flinty, of a yellowish white colour, sometimes red, and sometimes speckled.

It is contained in ears from eight to sixteen inches long, and from four to seven inches in circumference. In the middle is a hard substance called a cob, on which the grains grow close together, at right angles from it, and not obliquely like wheat, barley, or rye.

On each ear there are always either twelve or sixteen rows, and the whole is covered with a thick strong white husk, composed of three or four leaves or coats, which adhere to the whole very closely, and are each something more than the whole ear in length, to which they are united at the stalk, or lower extremity.

Indian corn is neither sown, nor reaped. It is planted and gathered.

The ground for it, is first plowed over one way, quite flush; this is crossed by furrows five or six feet asunder, and these by other furrows at right angles at similar distances, which divide the whole field into squares of five or six feet every way.

In each crossing, three grains of corn are dropped, and covered with a hand hoe; this is performed some time in the month of May, and is termed *Planting of Corn*.

After it has sprung up above the ground, when any is missing, or not come up, proceeding either from bad seed, or worms, vermin, and insects that destroy the tender shoots, the hills are supplied with fresh grains again, which is denominated *Replanting the Corn*.

It is afterwards plowed across the first furrows: the next plowing is across these; and

and so on alternately, until it is all plowed five times over; then it is weeded and chopped around the roots of the stalks with broad hand hoes; this is called *Laying by the Corn*.

In August and September it begins to blossom and shoot out ears, which is called *To tassel*, because beautiful, shining, silky tassels come out from the extreme end of the ears, and hang waving down.

These ears proceed from the joints, from the height of three to six feet above the ground.

There is also another beautiful blossom at the very top of the whole, which is in reality the male flowers, or farina, as the elegant shining silky tassels are the female; for this plant is both male and female in itself.

These tassels are as soft as silk, and of all different colours appearing very bright glossy and delightful to the eye.

This state of it is denominated *The Corn being in Silks*.

It has been difcovered that the fine farina from the male flowers, being carried by the wind and agitation of the air upon the female filky taffels, impregnate them, and fill the grain in the ears; for there is a taffel or filk proceeds from every fingle grain; and experiments have evinced, that one male will impregnate five hundred plants, when all the reft of the tops, which contain the male bloffoms, are cut off, and only the female, or ears in filks are left.

It has been experienced alfo, that if there be a field of corn within a mile or two of one where all the tops or male bloffoms are cut off entirely, yet ftill the ears will be impregnated and filled by the male farina brought by the agitation of the air and the winds; but the ears will not be all full.

But it has likewife been difcovered by experiments, that if all the tops or male bloffoms are cut off in a field of corn, and there be not another field within fix or feven miles, the whole field will be ufelefs;

there

there will be no grain on the ears, which will not fill, becaufe the female part of the plant has not been impregnated by the male.

The height of the ftalks, when in a ftate of perfect maturity, is from eight to twelve feet and upwards; with joints at the diftance of eight or ten inches from each other, at each of which are two leaves or blades, from one to two feet in length, and two or three inches broad.

The male flowers, as has been juft obferved, grow at the top of all, and appear fomething like to the heads or ears of rice, or large oats, after the fine farina is blown off.

The female flowers are rather below the middle of the ftalk, at the extremity of the ears which proceed from the joints in that part of the ftalk.

In October the blades, or leaves, which are broad and long, are pulled off, and tied in bundles, being left in the field to cure, and are excellent provender for horfes; for thofe who are accuftomed to
this

this will not eat the very fineſt hay; then the tops are alſo cut off juſt above the ear.

And during the latter part of November, and all December, after the froſts have come on, the corn is gathered, two, three, and four ears from every ſtalk, and the ſtalks, each of which is generally above an inch in diameter, are left ſtanding in the field.

A buſhel of corn will plant near twenty acres; and on the richeſt lands twenty acres will produce two hundred and fifty barrels, or one thouſand two hundred and fifty buſhels. A moſt aſtoniſhing increaſe indeed!

The land is firſt plowed with two horſes in the plough, becauſe the labour is then harder; but every ploughing beſides is done with one horſe only; and one plough will work between thirty and forty acres in Indian corn.

The whole of this excellent grain is uſeful, and there is no part of it ſhould be thrown away.

The

The leaves cured are excellent provender for horſes; the tops, ſtalks, and huſks are exceeding fine fodder for cattle, and the grain itſelf ſupports the inhabitants themſelves, both white and black, beſides feeding their horſes, and fattening their hogs.

CHAP.

CHAP. XXXIX.

Set out for Kentucky. Visit the Summit of the Wart Mountain. Discription of a most extensive, grand, and elegant Perspective. Ideas raised in the Mind.

AFTER this long digression on the culture of Indian corn, the grand staff of life throughout this continent, I shall proceed with an account of my journey to Kentucky; for my white savage and I set out from the fort early next morning.

I had procured rifles, ammunition, and Indian dresses for us both, which are by far the most convenient for travelling in that country; as also blankets to cover us, as we should be obliged to sleep in the woods every night; besides bells for our horses, to enable us to hear them at a distance when they were turned loose to feed, and hobbles, or spancils, made of strong leather, and fastened on their legs, to prevent

prevent them from wandering out of our reach where we remained all night.

I myself was provided with pocket compasses before I came here, and had besides a very just idea of the geography of the country.

I must beg permission at this place to correct an error I have observed in all the maps of that country, which give the name of Smith's River to the Stanton, for this is a very great mistake, as Smith's River is that which in the maps is named the Irwine River; and it was on the north-east side of it, near the confluence of Beaver Creek, where the fort I just left was erected; the whole country round, for a very great distance, being now denominated Pitsylvania county, which is the south-western frontier of Virginia.

Having heard much of the Wart Mountain, one of the first, but most considerably of the Aleganies, or rather the Blue Mountains, for height, as well as for its amazing extent of perspective, I determined

mined to visit it, and ascend the summit thereof on my way; for which reason we bent our course towards it, and crossed Smith's River about nine miles above the fort, at a very bad ford, which was deep and dangerous.

After travelling through an exceedingly rough country, and in extreme bad paths indeed, frequently without any, as also crossing several deep creeks, or water-courses, we found ourselves at night beginning to ascend the Wart Mountain, which is upon the south-west side of Smith's River; and we alighted on an agreeable and convenient spot, near the side of a brook of water, to put up for the night, turning our horses out with their bells and hobbles on, to prevent our losing them.

We struck up and kindled a large fire, gathered leaves for us to lie upon, eat heartily of our jerked (or dried) venison, drank some brandy and water, (for we had brought a pretty large stock along us), wrapped ourselves up in our blankets,

kets, and lay down under a large tree, with our feet towards the fire; having travelled about forty-fix miles that day.

I cannot undertake to pronounce whether it is owing to the falubrity and elafticity of the air, thus in free circulation, and totally unconfined, but certain it is, that I never found myfelf dejected, indifpofed, or low-fpirited in the morning, after paffing the night in this manner.

I arofe in the morning as gay and chearful as a lark, and fet out at the dawn of day to afcend the mountain, with my mind filled with the moft agreeable expectations of the vaft pleafure I fhould enjoy from the amazingly great extent of the perfpective from the fummit, which is reckoned equal, if not fuperior to any, even the higheft and moft commanding inland fituation in the world, at a diftance from the fea.

As we approached the fummit we found the journey exceedingly troublefome, the afcent becoming more and
more

more perpendicular, until at length we were obliged to alight from our horfes, and lead them after us.

Even this we found the greateft difficulty in performing, and we fhould not have attempted it had there been any place where we could have left our horfes with the leaft certain profpect, or indeed probability of being able to find them again when we returned.

The height of the Wart Mountain may be about fix or eight miles; but the extreme fteepnefs thereof towards the fummit retards the progrefs of a traveller fo very much, that it is abfolutely a fevere day's journey to vifit the higheft part and return, making but a very fhort ftay to enjoy the beauties of the almoft unbounded and wonderful perfpective.

After many halts we reached the fummit of the mountain about eleven o'clock, and were then amply rewarded for the great perils and fatigue we had undergone to attain it.

Language fails in attempting to describe this moſt aſtoniſhing and almoſt unbounded perſpective.

The mind was filled with a reverential awe, but at the ſame time the ideas, and I had almoſt ſaid the very ſoul was ſenſibly enlarged.

The reflection on our own littleneſs did not diminiſh our intellectual faculties nor conſequence; and the mind would boldly ſoar over the vaſt extent of the earth and water around, and even above the globe itſelf, to contemplate on, and admire the amazing works of the great Creator of all.

In ſhort, the ſtrong, mighty, pointed, and extended ſenſations of the mind, at this aſtoniſhing period are far beyond the power of human language to deſcribe, or convey any idea of.

On the eaſt you could perceive the deep and broken chaſms where the rivers Dan, Mayho, Smith's, Banniſter's, and Stanton direct their courſes; ſome raging in vaſt torrents, and ſome gliding in ſilent gentle meanders.

On the north you ſee the Black Water, a branch of the Stanton; and the break in the mountains where the Fluvannah, a vaſt branch of the James, paſs through in a north-eaſt direction.

On the north-weſt you will obſerve with great aſtoniſhment and pleaſure, the tremendous and abrupt break in the Alegany Mountains, through which the mighty waters of the New River, and the Great Kanhawah paſs, the latter directing its courſe northward, a diſtance no leſs than two hundred miles from its ſource, where the New River meets the Green Briar river which comes from the north-eaſt, a diſtance alſo of an hundred and fifty miles.

After the confluence, being then named the Great Kanhawah, it proceeds weſtward inclining to the north, until it falls into the mighty river Ohio, after a courſe of more than two hundred miles from the junction.

On the weſt you can very plainly diſcover the three forks or branches of the Holſton, where they break through the Great Alegany Mountains, forming ſtriking and awful chaſms.

And ſtill beyond them you may obſerve Clinch's River, or Peliſippi, that is almoſt equal to all the three branches of the Holſton, with which it unites, after a courſe of three hundred and fifty or four hundred miles: the length of the courſe of the Holſton being alſo above four hundred miles before they unite and form the mighty river Hogohegee or Cherokee, which afterwards flows a courſe of two hundred and fifty miles in extent before it falls into the Ohio, to which it is at leaſt equal, in the vaſt quantity of water it contains, as well as the fertility of the ſoil on its banks, and far ſuperior to it in the excellence of the climate it paſſes through.

On the ſouth you can ſee the Dan, the Catawba, the Yadkin, and the Haw, breaking through the mighty mountains
that

that appear in confused heaps, and piled on each other in almost every direction.

Throughout the whole of this amazing and most extensive perspective, there is not the least feature or trace of art or improvement to be discovered.

All are the genuine effects of nature alone, and laid down on her most extended and grandest scale.

Contemplating thereon fills the eye, engrosses the mind, and enlarges the soul.

It totally absorbs the senses, overwhelms all the faculties, expands even the grandest ideas beyond all conception, and occasions you almost to forget that you are a human creature.

CHAP.

CHAP. XL.

Defcend the Mountain. Crofs the New River. Middle Fork of Holfton. Arrive at Stahlmakers. Crofs the North Branch of Holfton. Crofs Clinches River. Afcend the great Alegany.

I Remained on the fummit of this mountain until two o'clock in the afternoon, but was almoft as much furprifed at the inattention and difregard of the young back-wood's-man to the beauties and grandeur of the perfpective, as I was charmed with the enjoyment of it myfelf; for he went down along one of the fides of the mountain, and was abfent from me above an hour; in that time I heard the report of a gun, and when he returned he brought a fine wild turkey which he had fhot; and he earried it along with us in order to drefs for fupper where we fhould halt at night.

We defcended the mountain on the north-weft fide, and ftaid all night at the border of a beautiful fmall favannah or meadow, a little way from the bafe of the mountain, having turned our horfes out as ufual, kindled a fire, roafted our turkey, and made a delicious repaft upon it. What remained we faved for the next day's provifion.

We fet out on our journey on the following morning, and fteered our courfe as nearly weft-north-weft as the mountains would permit us, intending to crofs the great Blue ridge, or South mountain, through a gap that is only ufed by the hunters, which is about twenty miles fouth-weft of that which the great trading path goes over.

By this way we propofed to fall on the head waters of Little River, which runs into the New River juft above the crofling place, and thereby fave a diftance of more than twenty-five miles travelling.

In this attempt we were fortunate enough to fucceed, after a moft fatiguing day's journey of forty miles at leaft, and after crofling a number of large ftreams of water.

We

We halted for the night on the side of a large rivulet, which we conjectured to be either Little River itself, or some of the waters of it, having crossed the great Blue ridge at a most disagreeable and dangerous gap in the afternoon.

Here we killed another wild turkey, and dressed it for supper as before; indeed they were so very numerous that we could have easily subsisted a company of men upon them, and might kill almost any number we pleased.

Next morning we set out early, and travelled down the north side of the rivulet, which we found to be Little River, until we arrived at New River, and at last came to the ford.

The New River is broad, deep and rapid, frequently impassable, and always dangerous.

However we crossed it in safety, though with great difficulty, and hazard of being carried down with the stream, and we looked out for a convenient spot on the west side, where we now were, to remain on for the night.

This we found necessary to do, both because our horses were greatly fatigued in crossing the river, and also to dry our cloaths which had all been soaked in the water; although we had not travelled more than twenty-five or thirty miles during this day.

The low ground on the New River is narrow, but exceedingly rich and fertile; the high land is also very fine in many places, but excessively broken, rocky, and mountainous.

The timber on the high land is very large and lofty, and that on the low ground is almost equal to the prodigious heavy trees on the Roanoak, already described.

The New River, which is only the upper part of the great Kanhawah, not being navigable, nor indeed the Kanhawah itself, the extreme roughness of the country, and difficulty of access to it, the roads or rather paths being not only almost impassable, but totally impossible ever to be

rendered

rendered even tolerable, by any human efforts, will not only greatly retard the settlement of this country, but will always reduce the price and value of the land, be it ever so rich and fertile.

In the morning, our horses and ourselves being very much refreshed, we set out again on our journey; and after travelling ten or twelve miles, crossed a pretty large water course named Peak's Creek; and soon afterwards a large branch of Reedy Creek.

In the afternoon we crossed another great ridge of the Alegany mountains at a gap, and in the evening came to the waters of the middle fork of the Holston, where we halted for the night; having travelled this day near fifty miles, and over a vast quantity of excellent land.

Next morning we pursued our journey, and travelled down the side of the middle fork of the Holston, which we crossed no less than three times this day; and at night came to Stahlmaker's, where a few people, indeed all the inhabitants, had also
erected

erected a kind of a wretched stockade fort for protection against the Indians; but they had all left it a few days before our arrival, and returned to their respective homes.

Here we remained for two days at the old Dutchman's house for rest and refreshment for ourselves and our horses, which we had really very much need of, and also to make enquiry ocncerning our future route.

The land on the Holston is certainly excellent, and fertile in the highest degree; the climate also is delightful.

But the value of estates here cannot be considerable for many years, perhaps centuries to come, for the same reasons that have been mentioned to affect those on the New River.

Here we gained intelligence of a nearer way to Kentucky than that commonly made use of, which had very lately been discovered, viz. by crossing Clinche's River about sixty miles from Stahlmaker's, going over the great Ridge of the Alegany or Apalachian mountains, at a gap which had been used only by a few of the best hunters, and falling down on the waters of the Warrior's Branch, a river that runs into Kentucky.

With this route pretty exactly laid down we set out from the Dutchman's house on the third morning after our arrival, and after travelling over a vast quantity of exceedingly strong rich land covered with lofty timber, we reached the banks of the north branch of the Holston, crossed the river, and put up for the night; having travelled that day more than thirty miles.

The ford of this branch of the Holston is, if possible, worse than any we have hitherto met with, and is indeed extremely dangerous.

But we were so familiarized to danger and fatigue, as to regard any thing of that nature but little.

On the next morning we set out on our journey by the route which we had been directed to pursue, and at noon arrived at the summit of a vast chain of moun-

mountains which separate the north branch of the Holston from Clinche's River.

Here I had the pleasure of enjoying an extensive, wild, and romantic view, particularly that stupenduous ridge of the Alegany, or Apalachian mountains, which is the chief and most lofty of the whole.

It was rendered the more interesting to me by reflecting that I must cross it on my journey, our route being directly over it; and the summit of this vast chain was at the least sixty miles from the ridge whereon we then stood.

We made no unnecessary delay however on this commanding spot, but descended the mountain, and pursued our route with all the expedition we could; and we arrived on the banks of Clinche's River late in the evening, so that we could not venture to cross the ford that night.

This circumstance was a very great inconvenience to us, because we always got our cloaths wet in passing these great and rapid torrents of water, which situation is particularly disagreeable in the

morn-

morning, becaufe we muft either delay our time by making fires to dry them, or travel with them all wet upon us, which is the moſt unpleafant of the two, as well as being prejudicial to health.

Thefe vaft ridges of mountains which we croffed rendered this day's journey extremely fevere and fatiguing both for ourfelves and our horfes, although we did not travel more than about thirty miles.

In the morning we undertook the hazardous tafk of fording Clinche's River, and accomplifhed it after feveral plunges, as ufual, over our heads; neither did we halt to dry our cloaths until noon, when we refted at the fide of a favannah, fpread all our wet cloaths on the grafs to dry in the fun, which was then intenfely hot, turned our horfes out to graze, and after finifhing a hearty meal, lay ourfelves down to fleep.

Here we remained for two hours, and then arofe exceedingly refrefhed, and purfued our journey.

On the evening we had reached half way up the ftupendous weftermoft ridge of the Alegany mountains, the laft, greateft, and loftieft of the whole.

Here we remained all night, concluding to attempt the fteepeft and moft difficult afcent in the morning, when our horfes were refrefhed and ftrong, and ourfelves alfo lefs fatigued; for we always alighted and led our horfes up thefe prodigious fteep, and perilous afcents.

CHAP.

CHAP. XLI.

Cross the vast Alegany Mountains. Fall upon the Warrior's Branch. Cross the Ousiotto Mountains. Impenetrable Thickets of Laurel. River of Kentucky. Arrive at the famed new Settlement on Kentucky.

WE pursued our journey up the mountain next morning, but the sun was several hours high before we could possibly reach the summit, notwithstanding we made all imaginable dispatch.

This ridge of the Alegany or Apalachian mountain, is indeed of a most stupendous and astonishing height, and commands a prospect proportionably extensive.

I took a retrospective view, with satisfaction and pleasure, of the vast chain of mountains beyond Clinche's River, which I had crossed: and I looked forward, with interesting anxiety and eagerness, towards the Ousiotto great ridge of mountains, which I had still to pass over, and were at least fifty or sixty miles distant before me.

The

The fummit of this ridge, the moft lofty of all the Aleganys, is near a mile wide, and confifts of excellent ftrong rich land, of a deep red, or a dark reddifh brown colour, with very large tall timber; and there are fprings of water almoft on the very fummit of the mountain.

But as foon as we began to defcend on the north-weft fide, we found the declivity exceedingly fteep.

Yet the afcent on the fouth-eaft fide where we came up was regular and gradual confifting generally of good land, and covered with lofty timber.

This north-weft fide was almoft bare of foil; the trees and all the vegetation poor, fcanty, and miferable; and quite incumbered with rocks and loofe ftones, which exceedingly impeded our way, and retarded our progrefs.

By thefe obftacles this day's journey was rendered intolerably difagreeable and dangerous.

But we forgot our toils, perils, and fatigues, when at night we reached the

waters

waters of the Warrior's branch, where we halted and remained until morning; having travelled about twenty-five miles during the day.

At the enfuing dawn we again renewed our journey, directing our courfe down the Warrior's branch until we reached the foot of the great ridge of the Ouafiotto mountains, where we put up for the night; having travelled above thirty miles this day.

On the morning following we began to afcend the mountain, and reached the fummit in about three hours.

This laft chain of mountains is covered with laurel, and fo exceffively thick in many places as to be abfolutely impenetrable.

Here the great mafs of mountains terminated on the north-weft; excepting fome fpurs of the mountains that fometimes extended feveral miles into the more champaign country.

The fummit of this ridge is not more than a quarter of a mile over, and the ground as well as the growth of the timber is very poor and miserable, being almoſt entirely covered with univerſal and impenetrable thickets of laurel.

From the brow or edge of the ſummit, looking back we could ſee the huge Alegany mountains which we had croſſed; and on the other edge of the ſummit, as we advanced, I was delighted with a view, novel indeed to me at this time, and uncommonly beautiful and pleaſing. For the eye was now relieved from being conſtantly filled with the vaſt exuberances of nature, which alone it had beheld for ſo many days, by viewing a beautiful champaign country, covered with prodigious woods 'tis true, but at the ſame in full verdure, and interſected with vaſt rivers, and prodigious water-courſes, which all terminate in the mighty majeſtic Ohio.

Some of the courſe of this amazing and moſt beautiful river was alſo to be diſcovered by a chaſm or break in the woods, where it flowed in awful ſolemn ſilence.

I en-

I enjoyed infinite delight in viewing the beauties of the perspective here for a considerable time, and at last left it with equal pleasure, eager to penetrate into that beautiful country, which I had beheld with such delicious gratification at a distance.

I descended the Ouasiotto mountains, and in a short time fell into the great War path, which has been used by the Indians time out of mind.

This afforded me very great satisfaction, for the road was now much better than any I had travelled in ever since I had first entered the mountains, and thereby enabled me to gain greater distances in each day's journey.

But although we had now left the mountains, and although before when I beheld all this country to the westward of them it appeared as a beautiful level extended far beyond the view, and all the horizon was as straight and even as a line, or as the ocean itself, yet now we had descended into it we found it extremely broken, with abundance of rocks, and thickly intersected with water-courses.

However nothing could be more pleafant than the pure and limpid ftreams, that either glided along in fweet and filent meanders; or tumbled and dafhed from rock to rock, juft fufficiently to give pleafure without an alloy of fear or pain, as pellucid and tranfparent as cryftal.

I obferved that almoft all the rocks, not only here, but every where between the mountains, confifted of a blackifh grey lime ftone; and where that did not prevail, the earth, rocks and every loofe ftone appeared to be ftrongly and richly impregnated with iron ore, which certainly abounds throughout this inland part of America.

We flept that night on the banks of a creek, that runs into the Warrior's branch, at the diftance of about a mile from the river itfelf, as we difcovered in the morning when we went to look for our horfes to proceed on our journey.

The Warrior's branch is a confiderable river, and after its confluence with two more rivers, neither of which is fo large as itfelf, forms the Kentucky which is indeed

a very

a very fine river, wide, deep, and with a very gentle current gliding along almoſt imperceptibly.

The whole length of the Kentucky, including its meanders, from the ſource of the Warrior's branch in the Alegany mountains, to the confluence of the Kentucky with the Ohio, is certainly between four and five hundred miles, containing a body of land on each ſide, that cannot be ſurpaſſed, and ſcarcely equalled by any in the univerſe, for fertility of ſoil, abundance of game, excellence of climate, and every other beauty and advantage imaginable, excepting the difficulty of acceſs to it.

In five more eaſy days journeys, the particulars of which are not worth relating, as being not materially different from what has been already mentioned, we at length arrived at the famed ſettlement near the mouth of Kentucky, on the eighth day of June, after having travelled at leaſt four hundred and ninety miles, from the fort on Smith's River, to this place, in nineteen days.

CHAP.

CHAP. XLII.

The famed Settlement of Kentucky. Mr. Henderson no military Man. Injudicious Forts. A fine commanding Situation. Want of Subordination in America. Hardy Race, but illiberal. Elephants Bones on the Ohio.

I Was soon directed to the house of Mr. Henderson, where I found a most hospitable and kind reception.

We walked over his plantation, which was really a very fine one; and being furnished with fresh horses we rode round several of the improvements in the neighbourhood.

He recollected me perfectly, but appeared very much surprised at the hazards, as well as the fatigues I had encountered to pay him and his settlement this visit, at this critical time, which it seems had been apprehended by every one to be particularly dangerous.

All the inhabitants of this settlement had also prepared for an Indian war, having

having erected three stockaded forts, into which they had thrown themselves, their wives, and families; but had remained only a very short time within them, and had left them and returned to their respective habitations not more than about a week or ten days before my arrival, which totally dissipated all their remaining apprehensions of danger or distrust.

Almost every house in the whole settlement was built of logs, which are proof against small arms, but being covered as well as entirely constructed of wood, nothing would be more easy for an enemy than to set them on fire, which prevents any idea of defence against such numbers as might be able to approach close to them.

The three stockaded forts also, though intended to cover the country against the attacks of the Indians, were neither calculated for that purpose, nor indeed were they tenable against an enemy of the least military knowledge, whose power or force might enable them to command the open country; for neither of the forts either communicated with, nor supported the other, at least what they intended as means of communication and support defeated the very purpose they expected it to promote.

The impropriety and total unfitness of these forts as places of defence I soon convinced Mr. Henderson of, as well as the rest of the principal inhabitants, and pointed out a commanding spot of ground to erect a fortification on, if ever they should again have such an occasion; which was indeed absolutely necessary, in their situation, for every reason.

It was a peninsula, containing above an hundred acres of rich low land, surrounded with the river Kentucky, and a large creek, on three sides, and on the neck of the peninsula, or rather just within it, there was a remarkably high and steep hill, which appeared to be composed of a solid rock very slightly covered with soil, but abundantly with loose stones.

Just

Juft before the neck of the peninfula, in a fmall circle round the bottom of the hill, there was a large morafs or fwamp, broad, deep and miry, which was covered and overflowed with water, after heavy rains, as well as during the periodical floods of the Kentucky.

In fhort nature feemed to have formed this commanding eminence for a moft delightful feat, as well as for the purpofe of defence; and it required but very little affiftance of art to render it extremely ftrong.

Mr. Henderfon was beyond all doubt a man of a vaft and enterprifing genius; he might be an excellent judge, as well as a great legiflator; but he was certainly not at all calculated for arms, being void of any talents that way, and totally deficient even of a military eye, judgment, or difpofition.

I have obferved that throughout all the back country, indeed I had almoft faid throughout all America, there feems to be be no such thing as any idea of subordination, or difference of ranks in life; excepting from the weaker to the stronger; and from the slaves to the whites.

In any of their forts it was all anarchy and confusion, and you could not discover what person commanded, for in fact no person did actually command entirely.

This total want of subordination renders the whole country particularly disagreeable to strangers, such especially as have been accustomed to the polished intercourse of Europe; for in the back-woods, and frontiers especially, there is no degree of insolence, impertinence and rudeness but they think themselves justifiable in practising, either to one another, or towards such as may come among them, and in a manner, as well as to an extent, that could not be credited by Europeans, had not so many seen and experienced it.

Mr. Henderson had epitomised, and simplified the laws of England, for the government and internal police of his settlement.

Magi-

Magiſtrates were choſen by the inhabitants, but with his approbation; and ſuch diſputes as could not be decided by one or two magiſtrates were determined by ſomething like a jury, whoſe deciſions were alſo regulated, and indeed in a great meaſure directed likewiſe by Mr. Henderſon himſelf.

Although the inhabitants are in reality a rude, barbarous and unpoliſhed ſet of men, yet you will frequently find pleaſure in their converſation; their ideas are bold and ſpirited, but their ſentiments are not liberal.

However, they are certainly a ſenſible, enterpriſing, hardy, unpoliſhed race, yet open, free and hoſpitable.

Puſillanimouſneſs, cowardice and mean ſpirit appear not there; hitherto they have not reached ſo far, and as yet are generally confined on the eaſt of the mountains.

In our rides through, and around this ſettlement we viſited the confluence of the Kentucky with the Ohio, and ſtrolled for many miles on the banks of the laſt mentioned river alſo.

Near the confluence is the place on the banks of the Ohio where the ſkeletons of nine elephants, as they are called, though many ſay erroneouſly, were diſcovered; which has given riſe to ſuch multitudes of conjectures among the naturaliſts and philoſophers, without one of them being able to account for this very ſingular and extraordinary circumſtance in a manner reconcilable to common ſenſe and reaſon.

For there certainly is none of the ſpecies (of elephants) now in the whole continent of North and South America.

It has been lately denied that they are the bones of elephants; and they are aſſerted to be the bones of ſome other very large animal, of which likewiſe at preſent none of the ſpecies is to be found.

I would not venture to pronounce upon my weak judgment, whether they are the bones of elephants or not, I mean

United States of America. 333

thofe few that I faw there, however I am very certain that they are much larger than belong to any other quadruped in the world, that I ever faw or heard of.

But to what fpecies they did belong, or in what manner they came there, is more than I can undertake to afcertain, or even to guefs at.

CHAP.

CHAP. XLIII.

The Rivers Kentucky and Ohio. Woods and Inclosures. Game. Wild Beasts and Fish. A general Account of the Indians. Their Character. Dispositions and Numbers.

THE breadth of the Kentucky at the confluence is between three and four hundred yards; and that of the Ohio between eight hundred and nine hundred yards.

The low ground on both rivers is excellent; on the Ohio it is about a mile wide; on the Kentucky about half as much.

The high land also between the rivers is exceedingly rich, and of a reddish brown colour, with large lofty straight timber.

The soil of the low grounds is a very dark brown, almost a black.

The woods consist of walnut, poplar yellow and white, red-bud, hiccory, saffafras, wild cherry, oak, of many different kinds, such as red oak, Spanish oak, white-oak,

oak, black oak, scrubby oak or black-jacks, chesnut-oak, willow-oak, and live-oak, maple, black gum, sweet gum, sycamore, horn-beam, dog-wood, pine, chesnut, beech, holly, maple, cedar, and many other kinds peculiar to the country, all of an astonishing size, especially in the low grounds, many trees being twelve and fifteen feet diameter in the trunk.

These are useful in America for many purposes; for houses, which are almost all constructed, and even covered entirely with wood; as also for fences and inclosures, these being all composed of what is called there *fence rails*, which are made out of trees cut or sawed into lengths of eleven or twelve feet, which again are mauled or split into rails from four to six inches thick.

When the inclosure is formed, every one crossing the other obliquely at each end, in regular succession and erection, these rails are laid zig-zag upon each other for ten or eleven rails in height, then stakes are put against each corner double across each other, with the lower end sunk a little into the earth,
and

and above thefe ftakes, one, and fometimes two more rails are laid, which lock up the whole, and keep it fteady and firm.

Thefe inclofures are generally feven, eight and nine feet high, and are very ftrong, as well as convenient, as they can be removed at any time to any other place where they may become more neceffary.

Timber alfo ferves for fuel, as no other is made ufe of, all over America.

The Ohio here has two banks on each fide; when the river is low, the waters are confined within the loweft banks; at this time the batteaux come up the ftream, which is then fmooth and gentle.

But when the periodical floods happen, which are always twice a year, the river is then fwelled to the higheft part of the upper banks, and runs with much greater rapidity and force, batteaux and veffels of all kinds then defcend with the ftream, and frequently attain the diftance of an hundred miles a day.

At fuch times, fhips of fmall burthen might go down from Pittfburg to New Orleans,

Orleans, &c. in the greateſt ſafety, there being then ſeldom leſs than twenty-five feet water.

Theſe laſt banks the river very ſeldom, or never overflows, therefore the land is little liable to be flooded.

Fiſh are innumerable in the rivers here, ſuch as perch, pike, eels, trout, roch, ſhads, old-wives, cat-fiſh, &c. &c. very fat, and ſo aſtoniſhingly large, credibility is endangered in relating it, for it is a fact, that of the cat-fiſh ſome are from twelve to eighteen inches between the eyes, and they are eaſily caught.

Game of all kinds is alſo exceedingly plenty; a man may kill ſix or eight deer every day, which many do merely for their ſkins, to the great injury and deſtruction of the ſpecies, and to the prejudice and public loſs of the community at large.

Wild turkeys, very large and fat, are almoſt beyond number, ſometimes five thouſand in a flock, of which a man may kill juſt as many as he pleaſes.

Elks are also very plenty, as well as racoons, oppossums, foxes and wolves. All these are found in the lofty woods, while in the savannahs or meadows buffaloes abound. And on the rivers multitudes of almost every kind of water fowl.

There was another animal that particularly engaged my attention, it being one of the same species that formerly I just had a glimpse of among the rocks at the falls of James River, when it struck me with the strange idea of its resembling a fiddle with feet.

These animals are called here *Tarapens*, and are both of the land and water kinds. They are all however of the species of the turtle.

One kind of them bites very fiercely when incensed, and keeps his hold so tenaciously that he will suffer decapitation before he quits it; these are called *Snapping Turtles*: but every species of these animals is so generally and perfectly known as to need no particular description here.

Some of them however are extremely beautiful, and are adorned with all the elegance of the brighteſt colouring, and the moſt fanciful engravings, or lines in regular and exact uniformity: this kind is perfectly inoffenſive and harmleſs, nor are they larger than two or three pounds weight.

Theſe animals will live, it is ſaid, for ſeveral hundred years. [See chap. vii. pages 51 and 52.]

During a ſtay of ſix weeks, I made many excurſions in the country around, and ſometimes went very conſiderable diſtances, ſo as to take ſeveral days in going and returning; and they were chiefly by water, on the Ohio, and its branches.

Finding every thing in tranquillity, and the Indians perfectly quiet and friendly, I accompanied a Mr. Mac Gowan to one of the Shawneſe towns, and another time to one of the neareſt towns of the Miniamis or Tweetwees.

Both theſe excurſions were by water; and I found that there was ſcarcely any variety in the manner of living and cuftoms of the different Indian nations or tribes; for feeing one nation will enable a perfon to form a very juft and exact judgment of all the reft.

So that the defcription already given, of the Catawba Towns, reduced and enervated as they are, is an exact reprefentation of the Shawnefe, Miniamis, &c. as well as every other nation of thefe kind of Indians. [See chap. xxv. page 195.]

However fome farther general obfervations on the different tribes and nations of Indians in North America may not be unacceptable here; but it is rather a difficult tafk for me to give the proper and diftinct account of every different nation, and their refpective characters, &c. friendly or otherwife, (their general character and difpofitions, as I have juft remarked, being pretty much the fame), being not only unacquainted with their language, but having never been longer than a few days together in their towns myfelf.

So

So what I relate must consequently be chiefly from the information of others; however it is from such authority as I judge may be depended upon.

The general character of the Indians is, that they are crafty, sensible, resolute, very suspicious, and very vindictive.

An Indian will travel on foot five hundred miles, through the woods, in night and darkness, secreting himself during the day to revenge an injury done to his relation, or to any one of his tribe.

However in every thing, but their cruel and revengeful disposition, I admire and respect the real character of the native uncivilized and uncorrupted Indians.

Their sentiments, with all the disadvantages of poor inexpressive language, and of what is worse, a flat, dull, and deficient interpretation, contain and convey the most elevated, noble, spirited, and just ideas, delivered in that beautiful and elegant simplicity and allegorical figures of explanation, which add dignity and grace to the subject, and are so much admired in the Bible and sacred scriptures of the Christians, in the Jewish Talmud, the Mahometan Alcoràn, and in all the oriental writings.

Their sensual appetites however they have no great command of, especially inebriation, which they are particularly addicted to.

But the truth is, they are corrupted by the whites; for they copy after, and fall into *our vices, these* appearing in the most conspicuous point of view; and I am afraid that our external *virtues* are so *few*, and even those so *difficult to be discovered*, that the poor Indians cannot distinguish any of them to follow after.

They have also been so treacherously and barbarously massacred by the whites, and so often deceived by them, that the memory thereof is carefully preserved, and handed down from father to son, in order to keep the rising race sufficiently on their guard against our future snares and treacherous designs.

This

This I look upon to be the true cause of the great caution, and complete diffimulation the Indians are become so perfectly masters of.

Indeed they have arrived at so eminent a degree of duplicity, and disguising their sentiments and intentions, that without the assistance of the arts of writing, reading, or committing their thoughts and transactions to record, they far excel us at our own weapons of subtilty, craft, and precaution.

In short they are zealous steady friends; but rigorous implacable enemies, until satisfaction or reparation be made them for the injury they think they have sustained.

However let their inclinations at this present time be either amicable or hostile, they all are not now sufficiently powerful, either to contend against the whites in arms, or to do them any other material injury.

Whites who behave to them with uprightness and affability are greatly respected

spected by them, and obtain an amazing influence over them.

But they muſt firſt be ſufficiently convinced of the integrity and diſintereſtedneſs of the perſon; after which they are more at the command of ſuch a man than of one of their own chiefs.

Kings they have none, and the principal men of their nation become ſuch by their merit alone. Than this there is no other precedence, or difference of rank among Indians.

They enjoy the ſweets of liberty and freedom in the trueſt ſenſe, and certainly are not guilty of the many iniquitous and ſcandalous vices that diſgrace Chriſtianity and Europeans.

Their numbers on this ſide the Miſſiſſippi are conſiderable.

From the Gulf of Mexico to the Lakes of Canada incluſive, it is computed there may be about thirty-five thouſand warriors.

Beyond the Miſſiſſippi they are much more numerous, and many people, that have travelled there, say they are very open and hospitable.

The little intercourse between them, in that distant country, and Europeans, renders them less suspicious, less subtle and designing, and not so cruel and vindictive as those on the eastern side of that extensive river, whose greater experience, communication and transactions with the whites produce those pernicious effects. A reproach more severe upon us than on them.

Here I must beg leave to make one particular observation; lest, from what has been said, it should be thought that the Indians have a particular dislike to Europeans more than to the whites born in America; but the very reverse of this is the truth, for it is the white natives of the country that the Indians have the greatest aversion to, and by whom they have been so often most treacherously and barbarously used.

The white Americans also have the most rancorous antipathy to the whole race

race of Indians; and nothing is more common than to hear them talk of extirpating them totally from the face of the earth, men, women, and children.

The Indians indeed do not appear to entertain any dislike to the British or French, I mean those that are natives of Europe; nor have the real British or French any particular aversion to them, as the British Americans have.

CHAP. XLIV.

A List of the Names of all the different Indian Nations on the Continent of North-America, with their Situations, and the Number of Gun-men or Warriors in each Nation.

THE names of the different Indian nations in North America, with the numbers of their fighting men, from the best authority I have been able to collect, are as follow:

Names of the Nations.	Situation.	Warriors.
The Choctaws or Flatheads	On the Mobile and Mississippi	4500
The Natches		150
The Chickesaws		750
The Cherokees, behind South-Carolina		2500
The Catawbas, between North and South-Carolina		150
The Piantias, a wandering tribe on both sides of the Mississippi		800
The Kasquuasquias, or Illinois in general, on the Illinois river, and between the Ouabache and the Mississippi		600

Names of the Nations.	Situation.	Warriors.
The Piankifhaws	} On the Ouabache	250
The Ouachtenons		400
The Kikapous		300
The Shawnefe, on the Siotto		500
The Delawares, on the weft of the Ohio		300
The Miamis, on the Mifamis river falling into Lake Erie and the Miniamis		350
The upper Creeks, back of Georgia		
The middle Creeks, behind Weft-Florida	}	4000
The lower Creeks, in Eaft-Florida		
The Caouitas, on the eaft of the river Alibamous		700
The Alibamous, on the weft of the Alibamous		600
The Akanfaws, on the Akanfaw river falling into the Miffiffippi on the weft fide		2000
The Ajoues, north of the Miffouri		1000
The Paddoucas, weft of the Miffiffippi		500
The white Panis	} South of the Miffouri	2000
The freckled or pricked Panis		2900

The

Names of the Nations.	Situation.	Warriors.
The Canſes	⎫ South of	1600
The Oſages	⎬ the	600
The Grandes Eaux	⎭ Miſſouri	1000
The Miſſouri, upon the river Miſſouri		3000
The Sioux of the woods	⎫ towards the	1800
The Sioux of the meadows	⎬ heads of the ⎭ Miſſiſſippi	2500
The Blancs, Barbus, or white Indians with beards - - - -		1500
The Affiniboils	⎫ far north near the lakes of the ſame name	1500
The Chriſtaneaux	⎭	3000
The Ouiſçanſins, on a river of that name that falls into the Miſſiſſippi in the eaſt ſide - - -		550
The Maſcoutens	⎫	500
The Sakis	⎬ South of Puans Bay	400
The Mechecouakis	⎭	250
Folle Avoine, or the Wildoat Indians	⎫ Near Pucans Bay	350
The Pucans	⎭	700
The Powtewatamis; near St. Joſeph's River, and Detroit - -		350

The

350   *A Tour in the*

Names of the Nations.	Situation.	Warriors.
The Meſſeſagues, or River Indians, being wandering tribes on the Lakes Huron and Superior	– –	2000
The Ottahwas } Near the Lakes Superior and Michigan		900
The Chipwas }		5000
The Wiandots, near Lake Erie	–	300
The Six Nations, or as the French call them, the Iroquois, on the frontiers of New-York, &c.	– –	1500
The Round-headed Indians, near the head of the Ottahwa River	–	2500
The Algonquins, near the above		300
The Nipiffins, near the above alſo		400
The Chalas } St. Laurence Indians, on the back of Nova-Scotia, &c.		130
The Amaliſtes }		550
The Michmacks }		700
The Abenaquis }		350
The Conawaghrunas, near the falls of St. Lewis	– – – –	200
	Total amount	58,930

This

This being the whole number of men fit for bearing arms, from hence we may be enabled to form some idea of the number of all the Indian inhabitants, men, women and children, on the continent of North America; which calculation, however, I am ready to confess can be but rather a vague conjecture.

There being fifty-eight thousand nine hundred and thirty warriors, it is computed that about one-third of the same number more are old men unfit for bearing arms, which makes the number of males come to maturity amount to about eighty-eight thousand five hundred and seventy; and multiplied by six will produce five hundred and thirty-one thousand four hundred and twenty, which I consider as the whole number of souls, viz. men, women and children, of all the Indian nations that are come in any degree within our knowledge throughout the continent of North America.

It is a most melancholy consideration to reflect, that these few are all that remain of the many millions of natives, or aboriginal inhabitants with which this vaft continent was peopled when firft difcovered by the Whites; and that even thefe will foon be extinct and totally annihilated, confidering the amazingly rapid depopulation they have hitherto experienced, fince that (to them) fatal period, or æra of the firft arrival of the whites in America.

CHAP.

CHAP. XLV.

Leave Kentucky. Sail down the Ohio. The Falls of the Ohio. Agreeable Companions. Enter the Mississippi, and proceed down that River. Meet some Chickesaws. Their fine Horses. A gallant Nation. Attacked by a vast Superiority of French and Indians. Defeat them. Their Origin. Their Cavalry.

ABOUT six weeks after my arival at Kentucky two gentlemen from Virginia, on a tour from thence to New Orleans, called to view the settlement.

They came from Pittsburg, by water, in a very fine batteau which they had purchased, and intended to proceed in the same manner down the Ohio and Mississippi, being furnished with letters of recommendation to the Spanish governor of New Orleans, &c.

Having remained along with us at Mr. Henderson's some days, I discovered them to be uncommonly sensible intelligent

gent persons, possessing an extraordinary share of genius, spirit and enterprize, and was not difficult to be persuaded to accompany them in their batteau to New Orleans.

For I promised myself abundance of satisfaction and gratification in this voyage down the Ohio and Mississippi.

Besides I had been so excessively over-fatigued in my journey here, over the mountains, that I absolutely dreaded the thoughts of returning in the same manner.

For these reasons I embraced this offer with great pleasure, and after returning Mr. Henderson, and several other of the principal inhabitants of Kentucky, many thanks for their civility and hospitable entertainment, I embarked on board Mr. Wood's and Mr. Lewis's batteau, along with my young savage whom I brought from the east side of the Alegany Mountains.

This young man, whose name was William Fortune, solicited me most earnestly for per-

permiſſion to attend me this voyage, which I very readily granted, having hitherto found him of great uſe to me in every reſpect, and an excellent hunter and woodſman.

In both theſe offers I conſidered myſelf extremely fortunate. Firſt in my attendant, whoſe fidelity I had already experienced; and next in the company of theſe gentlemen who appeared equally gratified by having ſucceeded in perſuading me to undertake the voyage, and in being able to furniſh me with very tolerable accommodations.

My preſent companions and fellow-travellers were two gentlemen, the firſt named James Wood, eſq. who was member of the aſſembly of Virginia for the county of Frederick, was young, active and vigorous, was frank, open and communicative in his diſpoſition, and poſſeſſed a degree of candour and liberality of ſentiment, that rendered his acquaintance valuable in the higheſt degree; the other was Charles Lewis, of Auguſta county in Virginia, eſq. ſcarcely inferior to

Mr.

Mr. Wood in every estimable qualification and desert.

They had two Chickesaw Indians, and three white men in their batteau, and as they just wanted one man more to complete their number, my servant supplied the place.

However, although I now call this man my servant, yet he himself never would have submitted to such an appellation, although he most readily performed every menial office, and indeed any service I could desire; yet such is the insolence, folly, and ridiculous pride of those ignorant backwoods men, that they would conceive it an indelible disgrace and infamy to be styled servants, even to his Majesty, notwithanding they will gladly perform the lowest and most degrading services for hire.

At the dawn of day on the nineteenth of July we left the Kentucky, and had a very pleasant voyage down the Ohio and Mississippi, if one can give that appellation to such a one, where we slept every night

night on terra firma, or at the shore in our batteau.

We passed by the mouth of a multitude of fine rivers, and some of vast magnitude, that empty themselves into the Ohio and Mississippi.

On our right were the mighty rivers Ouabache or St. Jerome's, and Buffaloe River, besides a great many inferior in size, whose names we could not discover, that run into the Ohio before the confluence thereof with the Mississippi.

On the left, the following rivers empty themselves into it, viz. Rotten or Bear Creek, Reedy River, the prodigious river Cherokee or Hogohegee, Muddy River, Deep Creek, besides many lesser ones.

As we sailed down the Mississippi, on our right were the rivers La Sonde, Aux Prunes, Metchigamias Lake or River, the river St. Francis, the White River, the river Sotouis or Akansas, Red River, Piakemines River, besides a vast number of others, some of a prodigious extent, as well as many inferior ones, whose names we never heard.

And on the left side were the Kafkinompa, the Chickesaw, Prudhomme River, Maggotty River, or Margot River, Bayouc River, Soto River, Yassous River, Tioux River, Petit Gouffre River, Little River, and the Ibberville which scarcely deserves the name of a river, and is only known by being the Eastern boundary of the Spaniards, forming the island of New Orleans, whose territory, from the Ibberville Southward includes both banks of the Missisippi; besides a multitude of water-courses, whose very names we could not possibly learn.

The day after we left Kentucky we passed the falls of the Ohio very safely, by keeping well over on the right or north-western shore, for these falls are by no means dangerous; and after we had passed them we observed the low grounds on each side of the river widen very considerably, as well as the river itself, until we entered the Missisippi, where

where the land is so low that it is subject to frequent inundations.

After we had got some distance down the Mississippi, the high land, and sometimes the mountains approached the river, so as to render the low grounds on each side very narrow, which however were luxuriantly rich and fertile, even beyond a possibility of description.

There are likewise islands in many places, and some of them almost covered with reeds.

As we descended the stream of the Mississippi we observed several lakes, or as they are termed here *Lagunes*, sometimes on one side, sometimes on the other side of the river.

These lagunes generally had vast quantities of large reeds growing round the edges; and within them there were thousands of water fowl of every species.

Although there was no difficulty in killing multitudes of them, yet it was almost impossible to get them, because of the reeds, which rendered that part of the lagune, where they were, almost inaccessible.

These lagunes were formed by the vast body of water, that comes down in the annual periodical floods, forcing its way across the necks of many different peninsulas formed by the extreme crooked and meandering course of the Missisippi, and diverting the channel of the river itself, from its old direction around the peninsula, to this new one across the neck of it, by which means the place where the river formerly flowed becomes a large lake of standing water, here denominated a lagune.

One day while we were on shore at the mouth of the Yassous, a placid, beautiful, and noble river, a small hunting party of the Chickesaws came up to us, and at the request of our two Chickesaw Indians, as well as the others, we remained there two days along with them.

The Chickesaws are a very brave and respectable nation, not for their numbers,

for

for they are few, but for their virtue, and unconquerable spirit.

They are also remarkably handsome, and what is very singular, have a beautiful breed of horses amongst them, which they carefully preserve unmixed.

The Chickesaws, it is said, and I make no doubt of the fact, came originally from South America, having travelled across the continent for upwards of two thousand miles, and brought these horses along with them, which are of the breed of that much admired kind called Spanish gennets, having long since taken them from the Spaniards.

There is no Indian nation on the continent of North America near so handsome as the Chickesaws. The Hurons come next them in beauty.

The Chickesaw nation have always been steady friends and allies to Britain, and their fidelity was never shaken, although the French have often attempted it, by promises, threats, and the most formidable attacks with a force considerably

ably more than four times the number of all the warriors in the Chickefaw nation, either to detach them from the intereſt of Great Britain or to cut them entirely off.

In the former war, while the French were in poſſeſſion of Canada, they detached about ſix hundred and fifty regular troops, and more than two thouſand five hundred Indians from Canada and Illinois, againſt this ſmall, but heroic community, for the avowed purpoſe, and with poſitive orders, of completing a total conqueſt, and even extirpation of the whole Chickefaw nation.

They ſet out on this expedition with all the ſecrecy and confidence of ſucceſs imaginable, at leaſt in their own minds; but they little conſidered what ſort of men they were going to attack, and ſoon found, by dire experience, that no ſuperiority in numbers is equal to a determined valour and innate heroiſm; for the whole detachment was totally defeated, the French regulars being almoſt to a man cut off, and the Indians their allies faved only a fmall proportion of their number, by a precipitate flight, leaving behind them multitudes of wounded and flain.

This was the laft formidable attack made on the Chickefaw nation, either by the French, or the northern Indians; for there always has been a rooted enmity between the northern and fouthern Indians, who have been almoft perpetually at war with each other, without any real, and indeed without any oftenfible caufe.

But the Chickefaws have always been diftinguifhed for their gallant actions, and feats of the higheft heroifm, which has rendered them, even individually, to be particularly refpected throughout all the nations of North America.

For which reafon Chickefaw guides are more fought after, and are much more ferviceable than thofe of any other nation.

For although their language is not commonly made ufe of in any nation but
their

their own, yet it is underſtood by all, and among Indians is conſidered as the language of politeneſs and univerſality.

Another ſingularity that ſeems to be peculiar to this nation is, their frequently going out to meet their enemies on horſeback, which, with their very fine horſes that they take ſuch delight in, renders them in fact a nation of cavalry.

This indeed is the caſe with no other nation either in North or South America, unleſs we except the Patagonians, thoſe men of vaſt and uncommonly large ſtature, lately diſcovered by admiral Byron, and the other circumnavigators, &c. on the coaſt of Patagonia, near the ſtreights of Magellan.

CHAP.

CHAP. XLVI.

Leave Yaſſous. Arrive at Natches. Proceed to New Orleans. French Inhabitants averſe to Spaniſh Government. Inſurrection quelled. Earneſtly wiſh for BRITISH *Liberty. Number of Families in New Orleans and Louiſiana.*

ON the third morning we ſet out from Yaſſous River, on our voyage down the Miſſiſſippi, after taking an affectionate leave of our friendly, and as we really found them, hoſpitable Chickeſaws.

We met with nothing very material nor intereſting until we arrived at the Natches, which we did on the 20th of Auguſt, being juſt thirty-two days from the time we left Kentucky.

Here we ſtaid three days, and in that time received many civilities and marks of kindneſs from Major Fields and Mr. L. Claiborne, who were ſettled on very fine and valuable plantations, upon the banks of the Miſſiſſippi, having come there from Virginia, of which colony they were alſo natives;

natives; and we really found them to be very entertaining, senfible and enter- prifing men.

From Natches we proceeded on our voyage on the fourth morning, and arrived at New Orleans in four days, being on the twenty-feventh of Auguft.

Here we found almoft all the inhabitants were French; very few of them even un- derftanding the Spanifh language; and they entertained the moft rooted and im- placable averfion to the Spanifh nation and government, as well as a ftrong pre- dilection for the Britifh.

As a proof of this, although there is a penalty incurred, by proclamation of the Spanifh Governor, of four hundred or five hundred dollars, for even admitting a Bri- tifh fubject into one of their houfes, unlefs they immediately make government ac- quainted with it, yet they make no fcruple nor difficulty of receiving any Englifhman, and entertaining him in the moft generous and hofpitable manner openly; at the fame time taking care to enhance the efti-
mation

mation of their kind reception, by making him acquainted with the rifque they run, and the penalty they incur the forfeiture of thereby.

This is the general practice in the ifland of New Orleans, at fome diftance from the town, which however being the feat of government, and being alfo occupied with a Spanifh garrifon, it would be impoffible for the French inhabitants to fulfil fuch hofpitable intentions and purpofes therein with fafety.

They were at this time extremely mortified, humbled and intimidated by a circumftance that had occurred but a fhort time, at leaft but a few years before our arrival.

Soon after the territory of New Orleans had been ceded by France to Spain, the French inhabitants affembled together, in a large body, on the thirtieth of October, one thoufand feven hundred and fixty-eight, determined to expel Don Antonio d'Uloa the Spanifh Governor, and all the other Spanifh officers; accordingly on the fecond of November they fent them on board

board a large Spanish ship in the harbour with orders to leave the island immediately.

Previously to the above exploit they confined M. Aubry, who was Commandant while the place belonged to France.

The occasion was, the Spaniards wanting to introduce their commercial regulations, which the inhabitants refused to submit to, and declared they would be either French or British subjects, but never would consent to be Spanish.

The Governor and the rest of the Spanish Officers sailed for the Havannah, and left in the harbour a Spanish frigate with the marines, not in a condition to put to sea, and two hostages for payment of debts due to the French.

Four of the principal inhabitants embarked soon afterwards to lay a representation of their affairs before the Court of France, and solicit redress of their grievances.

Things continued in this condition for some time, but at last General Count O'Reiley,

O'Reiley, a brave experienced officer of Irish descent, (who claims the island of Jamaica in the West Indies, as lord proprietor when the Spaniards possessed it,) was ordered there by the Court of Madrid, and landed at New Orleans, with three thousand Spaniards, and three or four ships of war.

The inhabitants then immediately submitted; and General O'Reiley ordered thirty of the leading men in this affair to be executed, and confiscated the estates of about two hundred more.

This severity restrained their actions, but cannot command the will.

At this time so great is their desire to be under British government, and so general, so hearty, so rooted is their detestation to that of Spain, that only a dozen or two of Britons, of spirit and enterprize, would be able to wrest all that country from the Spaniards; as the inhabitants are all French, excepting the garrison which consists only of a handful of lazy, proud, miserable Spaniards, who despise the French settlers

settlers as cordially as they themselves are hated by them in return.

At this time there would be nothing wanting or neceſſary but to erect the ſtandard of Great Britain, and the French inhabitants would one and all ſupport it; ſo much do they wiſh for Britiſh liberty, and to ſuch a degree do they deteſt the arbitrary government of Spain.

The number of families in the town and iſland of New Orleans, and on the weſt ſide of the Miſſiſſippi, may amount to twelve thouſand at leaſt, all of whom are thus averſe to be governed by the Spaniards.

CHAP.

CHAP. XLVII.

Dangerous Alligators. Vast Fertility of the Soil. Spanish Beards. Wait on the Governor. New Orleans. Great Distresses of some English and French imprisoned by the Spaniards in New Mexico. Vast Flocks of Cattle and Horses. Extensive Savannahs. A good Priest. Leave New Orleans. Arrive at Manchac. Coast along the Gulf of Mexico. Mobile, Pensacola, Apalachicola, &c.

IN the river Mississipi, and on the banks, are many very singular appearances.

In the river, and in the creeks, rivulets and water-courses falling into it, especially near the mouth, are large dangerous animals named alligators, from ten to eighteen feet and upwards in length; they are a species of the crocodile, and equally, if not more dangerous than those of the river Nile in Egypt; these also devouring men, oxen, or whatever else they can get within their horrid jaws, in that crafty subtle manner, so often described already in different authors.

These render it dangerous to sleep in open batteaux on the Mississippi, and on this account travellers are obliged to lie on shore every night, near to a large fire, which always prevents the approach of any beasts of prey.

On this river the soil is so extremely rich, and so luxuriantly fertile, that reeds grow even on the high land; a circumstance that I believe is not to be paralleled any where else in the universe.

The grand culture and staple here being indigo, this amazing fertility of the soil not only produces larger crops thereof than are obtained from equal quantities of ground in any other land or country, but also enhances the value of the quality of it, which is always greater according to the superior richness and depth of the soil.

Another very singular and striking appearance is a kind of moss, in long and numerous filaments, here called *Spanish Beards*, which hang in prodigious quantities, impending in hoary majesty from

all

all the large branches of the lofty oaks, fometimes touching the very ground.

These convey a venerable idea of vaft antiquity, and ftrike the mind with an awe, and a fenfation of reverential regard that can fcarcely be defcribed.

This has alfo its ufes, being extremely ferviceable and convenient to make our beds when we fleep in the woods; and it is clean, foft, agreeable, and abundant.

The town of New Orleans is fituated on the eaftern banks of the Miffiffippi, about ninety miles above Cape Laos or Mud-Cape, where that river falls into the gulf of Mexico.

The banks of the river are fo perpendicular, and the water is fo deep, that a fhip of any burthen may lay her broadfide to the bank, to land and unload, and is moored by a cable faftened to the trees on the fhore.

The river is above a thoufand yards wide, and the current runs all downwards, as the tide does not reach near the town; indeed the tide is fcarcely perceived at all within the mouth of this aftonifhing river, whofe waters, efpecially during the periodical floods, may be diftinguifhed in the gulf of Mexico for many leagues, fome fay above an hundred miles out at fea.

The ftreets of New Orleans are laid out in rectangular directions, the houfes are generally only one ftory high, yet many of them pretty good, and they may amount in number to three or four hundred.

The ifland of New Orleans is generally pretty good land, and all of it very low and flat.

It is about an hundred and eighty or ninety miles in length, but not more than five miles from navigable water at any place throughout the whole of it.

On the very next day after our arrival at New Orleans, Mr. Wood, Mr. Lewis and I waited on the Spanifh Governor; but being informed that he was engaged for that day, my companions declined fending him any of the letters of introduction and recommendation they were furnifhed with.

Thefe

Indeed these haughty Virginians were so extremely incensed at this refusal of admission, that it was with the utmost difficulty I could prevail upon them to consent to pay their personal respects to the Governor any more at all, or to send or present their credentials; especially as it did not appear to them, nor indeed to me, that he was really engaged at the time we received that message and apology of excuse from him, as we could plainly discern him, through a window, observing and making his remarks, as we judged, on us, while we were walking backwards and forwards in the piazza, in expectation of his answer; walking in that manner being a kind of exercise a Spaniard holds in great contempt.

However we were admitted on the day following, and were even honored by a very friendly reception; though I must confess that there appeared to me a stiffness and formality, in his Excellency, that indicated a distrust, and seemed to say that he could have dispensed with our visit; not that there was any thing personal meant to us, for the frequent proofs of civility, and even generous attention, we received from him afterwards, evinced the contrary.

But we imputed it to that narrow, illiberal, and jealous policy of the Spanish government, by which they endeavour to preclude all other nations, not only from any communication with, but even as much from the knowledge of all their American settlements as possible.

The restrictions of the Spanish government on commerce render the prices of all European goods here very much advanced, and they would actually be almost intolerable, if the inhabitants did not contrive to get many things underhandedly from the English, French, and Dutch, by means of an illicit trade.

Indeed almost all the flour that supports New Orleans is imported from Philadelphia, in vessels belonging to a commercial house there, viz. Messrs. Willing and Morris, who have obtained an exclusive priviledge, for that sole purpose, from the King of Spain.

From

From this the Governor makes a perquifite of twenty thoufand dollars annually, as all the flour, being confined to the King of Spain, is paid for by the Governor, who orders it to be diftributed to the inhabitants at the rate of a dollar a barrel, clear gain advanced on the price, after the deduction of all cofts and charges.

During the time I was at New Orleans, a gentleman from Maryland, who had fallen, by a very unfortunate accident, into the hands of the Spaniards in New Mexico, and with feveral other Britifh fubjects had been moft cruelly treated by them, arrived there.

Having at length obtained his liberty, for he had been a confiderable time very rigidly confined, he came to New Orleans, to endeavour to procure a paffage, either to Virginia, Maryland, or Philadelphia.

This gentleman, defcended from a Roman Catholic family in Maryland, was mafter of a veffel belonging to his brother

Atha-

Athanafius Ford, of Leonard Town, in St. Mary's County, and had failed from the river Potowmak, loaded with the French Neutrals (as they were called,) who had been removed from Nova-Scotia by the Britifh government on account of their ftrong predilection to the French intereft there, which at every rifk they were always ready to promote and fupport.

The veffel was navigated by Britifh failors, and was bound to the Miffiffippi, in order to carry thefe French Accadians to their country-men there, where they intended to fettle.

But having got into the trade-winds, and being unacquainted with the navigation of that part of the gulf of Mexico, after having been reduced to the greateft diftrefs for want of provifions, their whole ftock being exhaufted for fome time, having fubfifted on the rats, cats, and even all the fhoes and leather in the veffel, they ran into Bernard's bay, and landed at the mouth of Rio de la Norte, or Rio Grande, in the

king-

kingdom or province of New Mexico, inftead of the Miffiffippi.

Happening to difcover a horfe, immediately after their coming on fhore, they killed him for food, which was certainly very excufable in their emaciated ftarving condition.

They had fcarce finifhed their wretched repaft, when the veffel was feized on by the Spaniards, and confifcated for the ufe of the King; and they were carried, moft of them to the town of New Mexico, and fome to Santa Fé, the capital, no lefs than eighty-fix days journey within land from the place where they came on fhore on this inhofpitable coaft.

Here they were all clofely confined for fome time.

But at length the common people were permitted to go at large, in the day, on condition of their labouring for the inhabitants.

Yet the officers belonging to the veffel, as well as all the Englifh failors, were ftill impri-

imprifoned with the moſt rigid and barbarous feverity.

However they were alfo offered a limited enlargement, on condition of their figning a paper, written in the Spaniſh language, which however they privately contrived to obtain a tranſlation of, and found it contained an acknowledgment on their parts of having been guilty of the moſt unjuſtifiable and aggravated crimes, and of being treated with the greateſt humanity and tenderneſs during this their captivity.

This they had the refolution and virtue of refufing to fubfcribe to, although they were actually in danger of ſtarving and periſhing for want of neceſſary food.

At length a prieſt, poſſeſſed of more humanity than the reſt of the barbarous inhabitants of that country, having called to viſit them, took compaſſion on their extreme wretchedneſs, made them a prefent of a fat bullock every day, and intereſted himſelf fo effectually for them as to obtain their enlargement.

But

But so numerous were this man's flocks of cattle, as well as of horses, that although these poor unfortunate creatures received above an hundred oxen from him, yet they could not be missed out of the whole flock.

And Mr. Ford assured me that he possessed more than fifteen thousand horned cattle, and near ten thousand horses and colts, which were kept fat without any trouble the whole year round by the luxuriant pasture which that country affords.

For it seems the land there is not overgrown with woods, as in the rest of America, but is universally a rich meadow, abounding with the finest grass in the world, and intersperfed here and there with clumps or clusters of tall and stately trees.

I made no considerable stay at New Orleans, which to me as well as to Mr. Wood, Mr. Lewis, and Mr. Ford, was rather a disagreeable place; and Mr. Lewis and I set out in a batteau for Manchac, leaving both Mr. Wood and Mr. Ford there, who were about engaging a passage for Philadelphia in one of Willing and Morris's veffels.

It was five days before we arrived at Mr. Edmund Gray's near Manchac; but here I was moſt agreeably ſurpriſed at meeting with an old acquaintance from Georgia, along with whom I had been initiated into the the myſteries of free-maſonry, in my journey through North-Carolina.

His name was Allan Groves, and as he propoſed returning to Georgia by the ſame route as I did, we all agreed to join company together.

Having procured a batteau on the Ibberville, or Amit River, which falls into Lake Maurepas, we embarked, and coaſted along the lakes, viz. Maurepas and Ponchatrain, paſſing by the mouth of the Nita Albany River, the Tangepahoa River, the Cheſoncto River, and the Pearl River which is divided into two branches, called Weſt River and Eaſt River, when it falls into the lake or bay of St. Lewis; alſo the river Ookahootoo, the Chencala River, the Booka Hooma River, Hunting River,

Pafquagoocula River, Cedar River, Pines Bay, and Pool River.

Having touched by the way at a vaft many iflands, among which are Mattheuraux Ifland, Roebuck Ifland, Cat Ifland, Ship Ifland, Broad Key, and Dauphin Ifland, we arrived at Mobile point, at the mouth of the great bay of Mobile, which is formed by a vaft concourfe of mighty waters.

Here we made no ftay, but immediately proceeded on our coafting voyage; paffing the mouth of Perdido River, Efcambe or Jordan River, Middle or Governors River, Chefter River, St. Rofa River, Bay and Ifland, Chatahooche River, St. Andrew's Bay, River, and Ifland, Roebuck point, St. Jofeph's Bay, Cape St. Blas or Efcondido, and St. George's Ifland which forms the mouths of the river Califtobole, and of the mighty river of Apalachicola, which is the eaftern boundary of the province of Weft-Florida.

The

The lands in this province are indeed most amazingly fertile and rich, especially on the banks of the Miffiffippi.

Old plantations, cultivated by the French fifty or sixty years, produced last year, that is the year before I was there, from forty to sixty bushels of Indian corn to the acre.

The culture of every thing here is altogether by hand hoes, and manual labour of slaves, without the assistance of horses or oxen.

CHAP.

CHAP. XLVIII.

The Rivers Miſſiſſippi, Miſſouris, Illinois, Yaſſous, Akanſas, Rouge, Apalachicola, Mobile, &c. Colorado. North River, or Rio Bravo. New Mexico. Gulf of California. Mines of Potoſi. Acapulco. Old Mexico. La Vera Cruz. Diſtances of Places. Deſcription of the Country.

BEFORE I take my leave of the province of Weſt Florida, it may not be improper to give a ſketch of the courſes, extent, and combination of the rivers; the diſtances between different places, as well within the province, as on the weſt ſide of the river Miſſiſſippi, along the coaſt of the Bay of Mexico; as alſo the ſtate of the colony, culture of the ſoil, ſtaple commodities, and population, of Weſt Florida.

Weſt Florida is bounded on the ſouth by the Gulf of Mexico, including all iſlands, &c. within ſix leagues of the coaſt, from the mouth of Apalachicola to the lake Ponchartrain; on the weſt it is bounded by the lake Mauripas, and a canal a canal, or river, named Ibberville, that joins the laſt mentioned lake to the Miſſiſſippi, and by the Miſſiſſippi itſelf; on the north by a line drawn due eaſt from that part of the river Miſſiſſippi, which lies in the latitude of thirty-one degrees north, until it interſects the river Apalachicola or Catahouachee; and on the eaſt by the ſaid river, until it falls into the Gulf of Mexico.

Its greateſt length from eaſt to weſt, viz. from Apalachicola to the Miſſiſſippi, is about four hundred ſtatute miles; but its breadth is inconſiderable from north to ſouth, being in few places ſixty-nine miles according to theſe boundaries.

From Roſe Bay, and St. Mary's Bay, to the north line, is not more than forty miles, which is the general diſtance acroſs, as far weſt as the lakes Ponchartrain and Mauripas.

From the mouth of the rivers Califtobole and Apalachicola to the north line is eighty-five miles, which is the wideſt part of the province.

From

From cape Loas, or Mud Cape, at the mouth of the Miffiffippi, to the canal cut by the French from the Ibberville to the Miffiffippi, being the northern boundary of New Orleans on the eaft of the Miffiffippi, is about an hundred and eighty miles by land.

The wideft part of the ifland of New Orleans is from Turtle Point, and the Ifles Aux Affiettes, oppofite to Cat Ifland, to the Miffiffippi, and is not more than forty miles at the broadeft part, which is about thirty-five miles above the mouth of the river: then above that place, from lakes Ponchartrain and Mauripas, and from the Amit and Ibberville rivers, it is not more than five miles, in general, to the Miffiffippi.

The town of New Orleans is in that narrow part, between the fouth end of lake Ponchartrain and the Miffiffippi, about ninety miles fouth from the canal or river of Ibberville, and about the fame diftance north from the mouth of the Miffiffippi.

From

From the uppermoſt, or moſt northerly end of the Iſland of New Orleans, to that part of the Miſſiſſippi at the thirty-firſt degree of north latitude, is juſt fifty miles.

Theſe diſtances are in direct courſes over land, by no means following the meanders of the rivers, which would generally render them double.

This boundary, already mentioned, was that firſt eſtabliſhed for the province of Weſt Florida; but I have underſtood that the north line has been extended farther up the river ſince, to include the Natches, and the mouth of the river Yaſſous, to which laſt place it was carried back by Governor Johnſtone's proclamation.

From the upper part of the iſland of New Orleans to the confluence of the Yaſſous is about a hundred and thirty miles north.

From the mouth of the river Yaſſous, ſouth to Natches Old Town, is about eighty miles; from Natches, ſouth to Baton Rouge, and Fort Bute, is about ſeventy-

seventy-five miles; from thence south to the mouth of Hooma River, where it enters the lake Mauripas, is about seventy-five miles.

From the mouth of the Yassous up to the first considerable fork, which is on the west side, is about twelve miles; and the Yassous is navigable forty-five leagues from its confluence with the Mississippi.

This province, extending so far along the coast of the Gulf of Mexico, and along the rivers Mississippi and Apalachicola, being about five hundred and ninety, or six hundred miles, must consequently include a prodigious number of rivers; the chief of which, as well as of all North America and perhaps in the world, is the mighty and majestic river Mississippi, navigable to the falls of St. Anthony, which is computed to be eighteen hundred miles, and afterwards for a thousand miles above the falls in batteaux and canoes; having the richest lands, the happiest and most delightful variety of climates,

climates, and paſſing through the largeſt and fineſt country upon earth.

Where it derives its ſource is not known, having been traced as far as fifty-five degrees north latitude, and an hundred and ten degrees weſt longitude from London; being even there a very large river.

The country in that part is very flat and marſhy, and the Indians themſelves cannot tell how much farther north and weſt it has its ſource.

From that place it runs in a ſouth-eaſt direction to the forty-ſecond degree north latitude, and ninetieth weſt longitude; then with many vaſt bendings, continues almoſt a due ſouth courſe, until it falls into the Gulf of Mexico in north latitude twenty-nine degrees ten minutes, and eighty-nine degrees thirty-five minutes weſt longitude; having received a vaſt number of wide, extenſive, and mighty rivers, and having ſtretched along this globe in a direct courſe, which has been traced, above three thouſand miles;

miles; and including the prodigious number of its bendings and meanders not lefs than fix or feven thoufand miles.

Its name in the Indian language is faid to fignify parent of rivers, or eldeft fon of the Ocean.

It receives more than an hundred very confiderable rivers in its courfe, many of them fome thoufand miles in length, the chief of which on the eaftern fide are the following, viz.

Firft the Illinois, whofe fource is between the lakes Illinois or Michegan, Huron, and Erie; as the Miffiffippi itfelf, in one of its vaft bendings, approaches near to lake Superior.

The fecond is the vaft river Ohio, or Fair River, a prodigious concourfe of mighty waters, extending behind all the Britifh fettlements, whofe fource is almoft in New York government, being navigable in large batteaux within fourteen miles of lake Erie; fo that the French, before the conqueft of Canada by the Britifh, fent three thoufand men, with artillery,

military

military stores, baggage, &c. from Quebec to New Orleans; viz. up the river St. Laurence, across lake Ontario, and lake Erie, and down French Creek, the Ohio, and the Mississippi.

The Ohio itself receives above an hundred rivers in its course, some of which (particularly the Cherokee or Hogohegee) are equal to the largest in Europe.

The last river that falls into the Mississippi on the eastern side, that I shall take notice of, is the Yassous, a fine, placid, deep, and beautiful stream, being navigable near an hundred and fifty miles.

It takes its rise near the falls of the Cherokee, or Hogohegee River, and runs through the Chickesaw nation, receiving many branches, but none very considerable, in its course of three hundred miles to the Mississippi, which is in a direct line, or five hundred miles with its windings.

From the source to the mouth of this very fine river, it is a most delightful open country, with few mountains or hills,

con-

considering its inland situation, and is the happiest, and most excellent and agreeable climate in the world.

It is possessed chiefly by the Chickesaws, a very gallant, brave, and respectable nation, and firm Allies of Great Britain, as has been already mentioned.

On the western side of the Mississippi are many vast rivers, but none more considerable than the Ohio. However not one of them is so well known.

The largest is the Pohitenous, or Misouri, whose source has not been discovered, and whose course extends (perhaps) some thousand miles, before it enters the Mississippi, which is almost opposite to the confluence of the Illinois, only about twenty-seven miles below.

A large river north of the Missoury is the river Moingona, and still farther north is St. Peter's River.

South of the Missouri is the river St. Francis; proceeding southward, the next is the Imahans or Akansaw River.

Then

Then that most excellent, valuable, and delightful river, named Rio Rouge, or Red River, which is of vast extent, extremely crooked, placid, and beautiful beyond description.

The Red River receives two very large branches on the north side, named the Black River, and Ox River, and falls into the Mississippi almost opposite to Tonikas in West Florida: this is the last river I shall take notice of on the western side of the Mississippi.

The most remarkable places west, along the coast of the great Bay of Mexico, from Cape Laos, or Mud Cape, at the mouth of the Mississippi, is first la Balise Fort and Island, some distance west is Ensenada de Palos, then Woods Bay and Island, Ouachas Lake, Ascension Bay, Vermillion Bay, then from Ouachas Lake to North Cape are eight small rivers, and two lakes.

There is also an island at the Cape, in which indeed is the Cape itself, first discovered in the year one thousand seven hundred and twenty-six.

West

West of the Cape, the first is a small river, and a large bay named Jacdaiches Bay, with three rivers running into it; the next is Mexicana River, which some distance from the sea is named Adayes River; then a small but long island; then the river Floris; a long island; the river Magdalen; another island; and a small river; then Rio de la Trinidad; Dun River which falls into la Maligne River; Colorado or Cane River; little Cane River; and Guadaloupe River; Leon River; Rio del Vino; and Honda or Deep River, all fall into St. Bernards or St. Lewis's Bay, and the Bay of St. Joseph.

On the south-west of Maligne River M. la Salle settled in the year 1685, and was killed about three hundred miles up Trinidad River, in the year 1687.

On the river Sablomini is the town and settlement of Presidio; within the bay are five islands; and upon the banks of these different rivers and their branches are the nations of Killamouches and Allacappa, wandering Indians,

The

The rivers Guadaloupe and Leon fall into St. Joseph's Bay, on the south-west of which is a very long and large island named St. Joseph's island; and the rivers Honda, Del Vino, Sacro, and Nuces or Nutts, fall into a Bay on the south-west of it, forming St. Joseph's Lake or Bay.

On the south south-west is the mouth of the great river Bravo, or De la Norte, which bounds on the north and east the kingdom of New Leon, and is indeed a very large and noble river.

The next river of any note is Rio de las Palmas, which is named Rio de las Nacos at some distance from the sea. This is a fine beautiful large river, and derives its source within an hundred miles of the Gulf of California in the South Sea.

Rio de la Norte or North River is also a very extensive and charming river, considerably larger than the last mentioned one, running in a course about middle way between the Mississippi and the Californian Gulf, and the rivers Colorado, le los Martyres, and Rio Grande le los Apostolos,

Apoſtolos, or Del Coral or Blue River, which form or fall into the Gulf, but is nearer to California by five or ſix hundred miles than to the Miſſiſſippi.

Theſe vaſt rivers, eſpecially Rio de la Norte, and the Miſſouri, head very near each other, about the forty-ſixth degree north latitude, and the hundred and fifth weſt longitude.

I have thus inveſtigated the ſource of theſe prodigious and extenſive waters, on a foundation that may be relied on; and it will give power to form a more juſt and perfect idea of the country, by mentioning the diſtances theſe vaſt waters, and principal places, are from each other.

From Cape Loas to Bernard's Bay is about four hundred and fifty miles, thence to the mouth of Rio de la Norte two hundred, then to Rio de las Palmas is ſeventy-five miles, which make altogether ſeven hundred and twenty-five miles.

The courſe of Rio de las Palmas is nearly eaſt, and the extent of it about five hundred and fifty miles.

From

From the mouth of Rio de las Palmas, in the Gulf of Mexico, weſt to the South Sea, at the mouth of the river Culiacan, the beginning of the Californian Gulf, is ſix hundred miles.

From Tonikas on the Miſſiſſippi to Mexico, or Juan Baptiſta on Rio de la Norte, is ſix hundred and fifty miles; viz. to the croſſing of Red River an hundred and fifty, to Adayes ſeventy-five, to Trinidad ſeventy-five, to the Rio St. Marco is an hundred and fifty, to Mexico on the North River two hundred.

From Mexico to California, at the Bay of St. Lucas, Pearl River, or the Bay of St. Mary's near Cinaloa, or to Culiacan, is five hundred and ſeventy-five miles; viz. to the head of Pearl River three hundred and ſeventy-five miles, to the mouth two hundred and fifty miles, this being in the ſouth part of New Navarre.

New Mexico or St. Paul's is about ſix hundred miles, up the North River, from the Gulf of Mexico.

From

From Mexico, on the North River, to the mines of Potosi is five hundred miles, to Old Mexico seven hundred, to Acapulco nine hundred, and the same to La Vera Cruz.

From Acapulco to La Vera Cruz is three hundred miles, from Old Mexico to La Vera Cruz two hundred and seventy, and to Acapulco two hundred and seventy.

All this country, to the west of the Missisippi, is incomparably pleasant and delightful.

In the fertility of the soil, in the agreeable mildness of the climate, in the softness and salubrity of the air, as well as in the abundance and excellence of most beautiful water-courses, it is not exceeded, perhaps not equalled, by any other part of the whole immense continent of America. Indeed it can be surpassed by no country in the universe. The multitude of most elegant and charming situations that excel in grandeur and delightfulness of perspective, as well as the astonishing luxuriance of the soil, are far beyond any thing that can be conceived. There

There are also vast numbers of excellent harbours, and beautiful extensive navigable rivers. The earth pours forth every vegetable production in the most abundant profusion, almost spontaneously, and in a manner without labour. Black cattle, horses, and every useful animal, multiply to an incredible degree, without any kind of trouble, as there is no occasion for providing a stock of provender for them against winter. In short, there is no advantage, charm, or desirable qualification, that bountiful nature can bestow, but is heaped, with a degree of profusion, on this lovely country, that is not to be described in language, or conceived in idea. For it really is capable of being rendered, not only the garden of America, but of the whole world.

Yet this fine country is at present little better than an uncultivated desart, owing to the mistaken and narrow policy of the Spanish government, under whose absolute, and uncontrouled domination it has ever remained.

END OF THE FIRST VOLUME.

You may also be interested in these titles:

Townsends is please to make available a growing list of rare and valuable books from the 18th and early 19th centuries, including those listed below. Be sure to visit our website for a complete list of titles.

Cookbooks

The Art of Cookery by Hannah Glasse (1765)

The Domestick Coffee-Man by Humphrey Broadbent (1722) and *The New Art of Brewing Beer* by Thomas Tyron (1690)

The Complete Housewife by Eliza Smith (1730)

The Universal Cook by John Townshend (1773)

The Practice of Cookery by Mrs. Frazer (1791 & 1795)

The London Art of Cookery by John Farley (1787)

The Complete Confectioner by Hannah Glasse (1765)

A New and Easy Method of Cookery by Elizabeth Cleland (1755)

The English Art of Cookery by Richard Briggs (1788)

18th & Early 19th-Century Brewing by multiple authors

The Lady's Assistant by Charlotte Mason (1777)

The Experienced English Housekeeper by Elizabeth Raffald (1769)

The Professed Cook by B. Clermont (1769)

The Cook's and Confectioner's Dictionary by John Nott (1723)

The Modern Art of Cookery Improved by Ann Shackleford (1765)

The Country Housewife's Family Companion by William Ellis (1750)

A Collection of Above Three Hundred Receipts by Mary Kettelby (1714)

England's Newest Way in All Sorts of Cookery by Henry Howard (1726)

Biographies & Journals

The Hessians by multiple authors

Travels Through the Interior Parts of North-America in the Years 1766, 1767, and 1768 by Jonathan Carver (1778)

The Women of the American Revolution, Volumes 1, 2, & 3 by Elizabeth Ellet (1848)

The Backwoods of Canada by Catharine Parr Traill (1836)

Travels into North America by Peter Kalm (1760)

New Travels in the United States of America. Performed in 1788 and *The Commerce of America and Europe* by J.P. Brissot De Warville (1792 & 1795)

The Journal of Nicholas Cresswell, 1774–1777 by Nicholas Cresswell (1924)

An Account of the Life of the Late Reverend Mr. David Brainerd by Jonathan Edwards (1765 & 1824)

Travels for Four Years and a Half in the United States of America During 1798, 1799, 1800, 1801, and 1802 by John Davis (1909)

Travels through North and South Carolina, Georgia, East and West Florida by William Bartram (1792)

A Tour in the United States of America, Volumes 1 & 2 by John F. Smyth Stuart (1784)

www.townsends.us

www.ingramcontent.com/pod-product-compliance
Lightning Source LLC
Chambersburg PA
CBHW070525090426
42735CB00013B/2867